Cc

MW01234877

No part of this book may be reproduced, or stored in a retrieval system, or transmitted in any form or by any means, electronic, mechanical, photocopying, recording, or otherwise, without express written permission of the publisher.

ISBN-13: 9798690826581

Cover design by: Ann Carter
Library of Congress Control Number: TXu 2-225-029
Printed in the United States of America

FAMOUS CATFISH STEW

A young man's unexpected discovery

Andrew Carter Curtis

This book is dedicated to my sons:
Grayson Drew Curtis
Everett Cole Curtis

What lies out there for us today?

TABLE OF CONTENTS

"It's hard to adequately put into words how much this book means to me... Papa was right there on the page!"

"The way you described their place was wonderful, and I felt like I was right back there again with Papa in his shop and Mama Nell relaxing in her chair."

This book "is something to treasure and pass on to the next generations."

---AMY, MR. ANDREWS' GRANDDAUGHTER

I had come to a place where I was meant to be. I don't mean anything so prosaic as a sense of coming home. This was different, very different. It was like arriving at a place much safer than home.

---PAT CONROY

CHAPTER 1: THE FIRST VISIT:

"Cut away anything that doesn't look like a knife."

The first eager leaves anticipating autumn were boasting their colors in the bright sunlight, and the sky's depth of blue promised a cooler day. A mild breeze was revealed by the calmly swaying pine tops lining the road. As I rounded a sharp curve, I noticed a simple, old, white house positioned caddy-cornered to the rough, uneven asphalt road. An elderly man in a gray ball cap standing in the front yard was waving, hand above his head, while I slowed to veer left into the red clay driveway next to a small dark green pond. As I hopped out of my truck, the man exclaimed enthusiastically, "You must be Dr. Curtis!"

Accepting his firm handshake, I replied, "Yes sir, Andrew Curtis."

"I'm Edwin Andrews. Pleased to meet you. I'm glad you came over today."

Observing this man dressed in faded blue jeans, a blue and white plaid shirt with the sleeve cuffs rolled up his forearms, dusty, brown work boots, and a gray cap, I figured him to be around 80 years old. His shirt was tucked into his pants, which were cinched with a brown belt showing a decorative shotgun shell end cap near the buckle. A loose silver wristwatch circled the base of his right hand. His wide smile showed a dentured mouth below a down-turned nose supporting thin-framed eye glasses. Wisps of thin, gray hair protruded from his cap around his elongated ears. Wrinkle lines crisscrossed his face and seemed to accentuate his friendly smile. I felt like a giant towering over his small frame.

"Come on inside, Dr. Curtis. Let me introduce you to my wife, Nell."

Up a few concrete steps through a screen door which slammed loudly behind us, we walked on the small screen porch to a short, wooden door leading into the back of the house. Mr. Andrews rattled the finicky metal door knob and pushed the door open with a creak. As I stepped inside the once home of his grandparents, I was cheerfully greeted by a frail, slightly hunched, white-haired lady standing in the tiny kitchen. Clad in a matching white set of pants and long sleeve shirt imprinted with colorful flowers, Mrs. Nell instantly reminded me of my own grandmother. I leaned over to hug her neck and felt her thin, soft arms around me.

"Make yourself at home. I sure am glad you came to see us today," Mr. Andrews' wife quietly said to me.

I quickly looked around the kitchen, which was just large enough for the three of us to stand in comfortably. This kitchen contained the basics: refrigerator, stove, oven, sink, a few reddish brown wooden cabinets and drawers, and a small set of metal shelves with a coffee maker, microwave, and some pantry items. A single window over the sink facing south allowed a strong stream of sunlight to pour into the room and land on the tan linoleum floor. I was invited into the next room, the dining room, and instructed to take a seat at the dark wooden table along the left wall. Squeezing into position, my back to the wall, I sat down at the table waiting for the couple to sit too.

"Ever tried pepper jelly?" Mr. Andrews inquired.

"No sir, I don't believe I have."

Out from the kitchen, Mr. Andrews went to the head of the table while Mrs. Nell sat directly opposite of me. Before me he placed a dark, amber jar of jelly, a box of club crackers, a tub of cream cheese, and a glass of iced sweet tea. Silverware and a small plate at each seat had been previously laid out. Looking to my right, I could see a china cabinet displaying a plain pattern plate set and a small side table with a foil covered cake. A few flower pictures hung on the white walls. Observing Mr. Andrews spreading a thin layer of cream cheese on the full cracker followed by a dollop of pepper jelly smoothed down with a spoon, I repeated the process to create my own sample to taste. The combination of contradictions--sweet and salty, soft and crunchy, cool and warm-- danced merrily on my tongue like a song on my palate. Such a simple trio apart, but when eaten together a synergistic taste resulted. Chasing the treat with a gulp of ice cold sweet tea, I experienced the full taste sensation of this simple snack. I was hooked after one round.

The three of us chatted for thirty minutes, stuffing our mouths with the delicious snack, when Mrs. Nell suddenly declared, "You sure do remind me of my grandson. Doesn't he look like Mark, Edwin?"

Pushing up off the chair, she made her way through a bedroom door to my left and returned cradling a picture and beaming a proud smile. The picture she presented showed a boy of eighteen in a tuxedo, fairly tall with a nice complexion, dark parted hair, and an easy smile.

"This is Mark. He's a wonderful boy. So sweet and caring. You remind me a lot of him," she complimented me.

I felt my cheeks blush. "I would love to meet him someday."

"He stays on the go with his job," Mr. Andrews chimed in. "They send him all over the country for weeks at a time. Wish he had the chance to come home more, but he's a mighty hard worker, and I'm proud to be able to say that. Not all kids are that way nowadays."

After a brief lull, Mr. Andrews rhetorically asked, "So you say you are interested in learning how to make knives?"

"Oh, yes sir!" I almost screamed with excitement. "I especially want to make an antler handle knife."

Pushing back from the dining table, Mr. Andrews motioned over his shoulder to a doorway, "Well come in here and let me show you some I've made."

We proceeded into the next room, the den, where a plush, faded blue couch flush with the wall immediately on our left awaited us. To the far end of the couch was a small, dark wooden side table with a deep drawer and a short lamp on top. Mr. Andrews took his seat on that end, so I sat down to his right. I could see a sagging depression in the cushion on which he sat indicating years of use. In front of the couch was a long, narrow pine table with a Bible on top. To my left was a sealed fireplace with an electric heater inserted. Directly across from me were several large windows adorned with plain white curtains to block the eastern sun. A TV was positioned on a short, squat stand in front of the windows, and to the right angled at the corner sat a broken-in maroon recliner. Family pictures in small frames decorated the walls. Mrs. Nell, after cleaning the dining table, quietly entered the den and gently lowered herself into the recliner. Mr. Andrews twisted his body slightly to his left and opened the side table drawer with a scraping sound. He reached inside the open drawer to extract a knife bound in a leather sheath. When I saw the beautiful antler protruding from the dark leather, my excitement rose.

Before removing the knife from the protective sheath, he commented, "Now it's nothing special, and it's certainly not perfect…"

He slid the knife out and handed it to me. I was in awe at the simple beauty: the highly polished steel blade, the tarnished brass bolster (or finger guard), the red, white, and black spacers between the bolster and handle, and then the part that intrigued me the most--the antler handle. The handle was a solid piece of whitetail deer antler cut from the base of the antler. Dark yellow and smooth, it fit nicely in my palm.

"Mr. Andrews, this is as good a knife as I could ever hope to make."

"You will get there, Dr. Curtis, you just have to stick with it."

Pointing a finger at the knife I held, Mr. Andrews began a story. "That was the first antler knife I ever made. One day a long time ago I was riding out Gillionville Road out by Nothin' Fancy, and a deer had been hit in the road. I got out of my car to drag him out of the road, and when I grabbed hold of the base of his antler I thought to myself, this is a mighty straight antler. Ought to be good for a knife handle."

As I held the smooth antler handle in my right hand listening to the story, I laughed, "Yes sir, I would say this made a decent handle."

Taking the knife back from me and slipping it into its sheath, he returned it to the drawer and removed another knife, this time without a sheath. The simple, straight, small blade and matching brass bolster and end cap were overshadowed by the uniquely colored, smooth, polished antler handle. Unlike the previous knife, this antler was not cut from the base but from a section of one of the tines. The color and pattern, pale yellow with dark gray streaks running lengthwise, were different than any antler I had seen.

"That isn't whitetail antler, is it?" I asked doubtfully.

His eyes drifted towards the eastern windows. "No... I made this one out of a mule deer shed antler a friend of mine found way out in Utah. It was slightly bleached and cracked by the sun and surprised me how it looked once I polished it up. I don't think I could ever get another handle to look like that if I tried. Well, I did make a second one just like it cut from the same antler, but I've seemed to have lost it. Looked everywhere I know to look but can't find it. That knife I made to use, and boy have I used it over the years. Cleaned many a catfish with that knife. I have sharpened it so many times the blade's about like a toothpick. But this knife here," he said handing me the knife, "I made just to look at and keep in this drawer because it's so unique. And the steel I used on these two knives, well, let's just say it's unique too. The oldest steel I have ever used no doubt. And probably the best quality. Actually, I have one small piece left that would make a fine little knife. I have just been saving it for the right time..." he trailed off still staring out the window.

One after the next, Mr. Andrews displayed more of

his hand-made knives for my viewing, each with an interesting story. My mind wandered. I thought about the stories even before they were knives. The deer who bore those antlers. Where did the antlers come from? Were the bucks killed or did the antlers shed off in the spring? Were they from Georgia or across the country? Did Mr. Andrews find the antlers, or did someone give them to him? And what about the steel? Where did it come from? What was it used for before Mr. Andrews acquired it? When was it made? And the knives themselves. What had Mr. Andrews used them for? Some were so worn, evidenced by the light streaks from a whetstone. Others like the beautifully polished mule deer knife had never been used. Most of the knives were similar in basic pattern with slight variations to make each truly unique. They were simple yet beautiful. Beautiful yet modest. The simplicity made them more attractive.

Mr. Andrews, rattling me out of my daydream, enthusiastically asked, "You ready to go learn how to make a knife?"

He made the process seem so elementary in his nonchalant tone. Up from the blue couch we made our way through the house, out the creaky kitchen door, and onto the back, screen porch where the washer and dryer sat. The bright fall day greeted us and carried a faint smell of cut hay. I followed him out the screen door, allowing it to slam shut loudly behind me. Several cats at the base of the concrete steps scattered into the safety cover of the foundation shrubbery.

"You probably don't have too many mice around here, do you?"

He laughed, peering back towards the cowering cats. "No, it's got to be a mighty brave mouse to come around here. I'm glad because those dang rodents would chew on my deer antlers I got lying around."

I followed Mr. Andrews a short distance across the yard past a couple of old, towering pecan trees beginning to drop their yellow leaves and into an old metal and wood barn with a big sliding door and a red dirt floor. The inside was illuminated by nothing more than the sunlight coming through the gaping doorway. My eyes had to adjust to the dimly lit interior, but then I noticed a clutter of tools, some on tables, some on the earth floor and multiple deer antlers strewn about. Mr. Andrews opened a black and yellow toolbox on a metal table in the middle of the barn and retrieved two small, rectangular pieces of reddish purple wood. But then something caught my attention. In the toolbox lay about fifteen gorgeous antler handles already cut and partially sanded. I wanted so badly to look further, but I would have to be patient. Our lesson this day did not involve antlers.

"Do you know what kind of wood this is, Dr. Curtis?"

"No sir, I don't."

"It's purple heart wood. Comes from South America. It's really durable and polishes well. Makes a fine little knife handle."

Taking the dark wood blocks from him, my fingers stroked the rough surface as I tried to envision how this wood would transform to a knife handle. Next he grabbed a rusty section of a miter saw blade and sat in a metal-framed chair with a plywood seat positioned in front of a metal vice welded to a large anvil. Underneath the vice was a small red and white Igloo cooler with the top off and filled halfway with dirty water. A red solo cup floated on the surface.

He tightened the vice around the metal, leaned over to pick up a handheld electric grinding/cutting tool next to his boot, and said, "'Bout to get loud."

The grinder shrieked as Mr. Andrews maneuvered the cutting wheel through the metal to begin cutting out the knife pattern. The metal quickly turned a bluish color. Seeing that, he cut off the grinder and poured a steady stream of water from the cooler over the sizzling hot metal, allowing the water to land back in the cooler for recycled use.

My ears were still ringing when Mr. Andrews said, "You know the easiest way to make a knife?" He looked over his shoulder with a grin.

"How's that?" I responded.

"You just cut away anything that doesn't look like a knife!" He broke out in a rolling laughter that made me laugh as well.

"I have a feeling it's a little more complicated than

that."

He resumed the intermittent process of cutting and quenching the hot metal until a definite knife form took shape.

"Dr. Curtis, we are going to make a slab handle knife today. Ought to make a good little knife for the kitchen."

Once he had the basic knife pattern cut away from the saw blade, Mr. Andrews placed the tang (part of the metal that would go into the handle) in the vice, exchanged his cutting wheel for a grinding wheel, and began methodically grinding away to produce the cutting edge. Every fifteen seconds or so he would reach into the cooler at his feet to scoop a cup of water and slowly pour a thin stream on the scalding surface. When he was satisfied with the angle of the cutting edge, he shuffled to the wall of the barn where a rusty drill press was positioned on a metal table. No direct light penetrated the side wall of the barn, and I marveled at how Mr. Andrews could see well enough to work.

Drilling two holes about two inches apart through the tang, he turned to me. "You still got that wood?"

"Yes sir."

I relinquished the two rectangular slabs, and he coated a side of one with epoxy and pressed it firmly to the metal tang, securing the two pieces together in the vice.

Mr. Andrews let out a satisfactory sigh, "Ahh, well,

now we wait. Dr. Curtis, do you like to fish?"

The question struck me with excitement. "Yes sir! I love to fish. I started fishing with my granddad when I was three and have loved it ever since."

"Good!" he said through an amused smile. In the shadowy room his eyes seemed to sparkle. "Let's go down to the pond. I got some good eatin' catfish in there."

Stepping out of the barn into the bright autumn light, we headed back across the yard, under the giant pecan trees, and towards the modest white house. The cool breeze rustled the brittle, yellow pecan leaves overhead, releasing several for their single journey to the ground. A few leaves danced and glided down the path in front of me, catching rays of sun as they tumbled, electrifying their colors to a golden blaze. We walked behind the house to a white wood building, the paint severely weathered and chipped. Numerous old boards along the outer walls were cracked and pulling away from the structure. Four unpainted wood steps led unevenly to a heavy white door, which was propped open. The inside consisted of one fairly large square room with a small closet to the right, a high ceiling, and a large window facing south. A metal folding chair sat in front of two electric belt sanders. A dark gray gun safe and an upright freezer were on opposite walls. Between the window and the open door, ample light poured into the room.

Reaching into the closet, Mr. Andrews grabbed two fishing poles already set with hooks, corks, and weights and then bent down by the gun safe to get a light blue plastic can of worms and a darker blue Maxwell House coffee container.

"This used to be an old kitchen house back when kitchens were detached from the main house. They used to do that way back when to prevent fire from burning down the house if the kitchen caught fire."

"Was this kitchen a part of your grandparents' house here?" I asked.

"No, I bought this thing real cheap from someone down the road. They were going to bulldoze it down. I'm glad I got it. It's a good spot for my belt sanders."

Taking both fishing rods from him, I followed Mr. Andrews back down the four rickety steps and across the gently sloping hill to the small, oval pond. Just before the pond bank was Mr. Andrews' garden plot half filled with fall greens. The October sun glistened off the smooth surface of the water, the light breeze unable to produce a ripple but present enough to be felt on the skin. A single metal folding chair sat lonely looking out over the pond.

"That's one advantage of being a well driller," Mr. Andrews chuckled, pointing a finger at a small well pump spouting forth a continuous stream of fresh water into the pond. "My pond is always full!"

I had not known the man long, but already I knew that that statement summed up his psyche. I chuckled to myself; he was a "glass-half-full" kind of guy.

He set the worm container in the chair and twisted

open the coffee container. Reaching in, he grabbed a handful of brown pellets and tossed them underhand into the water. Almost immediately the water's surface boiled with lively fish in competition for the floating feed. One catfish propelled itself clear out of the water to land with a sharp, smacking splash.

"Next time I will have two chairs down here for us," he said almost apologetically.

"No problem, Mr. Andrews, I don't mind standing."

At that, he moved the worm can to the ground and plopped into the hard chair with a heavy sigh. Taking a plump, wiggly, pink worm from the opened container at his feet, he threaded it onto my hook, hooking the worm several times in loops before leaving a long end free to dangle. My granddad had been the only other person to bait a fishing hook for me years ago, and now at the age of twenty seven, I experienced a happy flashback of my boyhood days.

"Ok, Dr. Curtis, drop your bobber right over there... yeah... near where the water is flowing in."

As I did so, my cork plunged violently beneath the surface. I set the hook to feel the weight of a strong fish on the end of my line.

"How 'bout that, Mr. Andrews?! Feels like a good one!!" I proudly reeled in my catch, dragging it over the grassy embankment.

"Let me see him," said Mr. Andrews confidently. "I'll get him off the hook for you."

I watched anxiously as the elderly man snagged the lively fish with three sharp fins, gripped it firmly in his right hand, and then plucked the gold hook out of its mouth with a quick, easy pop of his left hand. He casually flipped the catfish into a white five gallon bucket.

"Catch yourself a few more, and you will have a good mess to take home."

The slightly angled sun rays reflected off the smooth pond surface away from us, illuminating the green, sagging water oaks on the opposite bank. I took another cast into the same spot. My cork made a soft splash and immediately dived under water.

"I got another one, Mr. Andrews! This one feels bigger!" He chuckled quietly in his metal chair.

After catching several more slippery catfish that partially filled the bucket, I realized that Mr. Andrews had not even made a single cast. With his fishing rod propped on the side of his chair, he had a look of contentment merely observing me.

"That ought to be plenty for you to cook," he commented peering into the bucket. "What do you say we go check on that knife? I bet it's good and dry by now."

So off we went up the sloping grass yard with the brittle pecan leaves crunching under our steps. I toted the white bucket of catfish around the old kitchen house to the backside where Mr. Andrews had built an outdoor sink. I dropped the bucket by the sink and followed him to the work barn where my partial knife was. My eyes had to adjust to the dimly lit interior of the barn. I watched as Mr. Andrews loosened the vice to release the knife. He carried it over to the drill press and drilled through the two holes he had previously punched in the tang and exited through the wood on the opposite side. Applying epoxy to the metal tang surface, he adhered the second piece of purple wood and again placed the handle tightly in the vice grip.

"Dr. Curtis, what do you say we go clean that mess of catfish you caught while we wait on this to dry?"

I followed him out into the bright daylight and gazed across the road at the cow pasture down the hill. The black cows were all standing and quietly munching on the browning Bahia grass. As if to acknowledge our presence, one cow mooed and encouraged a cascade of bellows from the fellow cows. The distant hardwood trees in the bottom echoed their calls.

Off to the outdoor sink we went. A group of semiferal cats trying to peer into our catfish bucket scattered in all directions as we approached. Mr. Andrews hurried into his house and quickly returned with a knife, an old wood handled one with a rusty, whittled blade.

"Did you make that knife?" I speculated.

"This ole thing? Yeah, I made it a long time ago... nothing special, but it will clean a catfish."

A dark, heavy hickory board balanced on the ledge of the sink. The wood was warped and cracked, and a large, rusty nail was hammered into one end, with the head protruding a couple of inches. Mr. Andrews grabbed a catfish out of the bucket, placed it on the board, and wedged the nail under the gills to hold the fish in place.

"See, I start to cut right here," he instructed, making an incision behind the gills. "That nail sure comes in handy and makes skinning it a whole lot easier."
"I see that. Looks like you've done this a time or two," I said laughing.

"I've cleaned many a catfish this way, Dr. Curtis."

I found it funny that he refused to call me Andrew. Out of respect for my degree, he only called me Dr. Curtis. There I was, over fifty years younger than he, and acting as a pupil in his teaching presence, and yet he called me "doctor."

A small gray tabby cat poked his head out from under the building. Mr. Andrews quickly tossed a string of slimy guts in that direction, and three more cats poured out to wrestle for the treat.

After cleaning all the fish, Mr. Andrews led me inside his house to place the meat in the refrigerator.

"You don't want to eat these tonight for supper, Mr. Andrews?"

"No, you take them. It's my birthday today, and we are going to eat Mexican tonight in Dawson."

"Well I had no clue... Happy birthday, Mr. Andrews!"

He smiled, "I'm 81 years old today. Born in 1931."

October 13--I committed the date to memory and

mulled over the significance of my first visit on his birth-day. He and I already seemed to have a deep connection, and I knew it was to be the start of a very special friend-ship despite the fifty-four year age gap.

My thoughts were interrupted when Mr. Andrews said, "Let's go finish that knife we started."

Out the house we went with the screen door slam-ming shut behind us. The sun was sinking lower now to our left behind the house where it was peeking through a tall stand of planted loblolly pines. The pine needles were lit to an impressive, vibrant green and softly whis-tled in the cool afternoon breeze. I paused for a moment while Mr. Andrews shuffled on ahead of me toward the barn. I realized that I could not discern any other man-made sound. The mourning doves hooted their calming melodies in the pine tops. The cows across the road in the sunlit pasture mooed contently. Next to a thick, gnarly muscadine vine, a young tabby cat sat on its haunches and meowed quietly. A lone crow flew directly overhead and landed with a swooshing sound high in a tall pecan tree. It crowed once before taking flight again. What a peaceful place! In a society of high speed productivity, where one's worth is often measured by efficiency, it is easy to lose sight of what makes us whole--the simple calm of nature. So mentally and emotionally cleansing. So simple.

I hurried to catch up to Mr. Andrews as he entered the barn. He released the knife we had been working on from the vice and handed it to me. The wood handle was a rectangular block and very rough to my hand.

"Now we got to put the screws through," he instructed. "I use these stainless steel screws I get out of water pumps."

He held up two screws for me to see. After using a tap to cut the screw grooves through the holes in the handle, he twisted the screws into their designated place to secure the wood grips to the metal tang interior.

"Ok, Dr. Curtis. Now we are ready for the final step. Let's go to the belt sanders."

Back across the yard we went to the kitchen house and up the four creaky wooden steps. Mr. Andrews sat in the metal chair facing his four inch belt sander and flipped on the switch, the motor producing a low hum. Taking the knife delicately in his hands, he pressed the wood handle to the sanding belt and began smoothing the rough corners.

"I see you are left-handed," I observed.

"Oh, yes sir. And that makes a big difference with what antlers I choose for my knives. You being right handed might not like some of my knives I use. But this slab handle here will fit nicely in either hand."

The block shaped handle began to take on softer edges as Mr. Andrews carefully twirled the knife against the sander. Once he was satisfied with the ergonomic grip, he cut off the four inch sander, rotated in his chair slightly to the right, and turned on a one inch belt sander.

Holding the smooth wood handle firmly in his left hand and his right hand bracing his left wrist, he pressed the side of the dull metal blade to the belt. Occasionally, he would pause to inspect the blade, which was becoming smoother and shinier with each pass.

The warm sunlight filtered through the open doorway and the large south-facing window. I watched the shadow of a pine branch twisting across the dusty wood floor in front of me. Peering out the window, I tried to locate the branch responsible for the shadow but could not. A mockingbird swooped in front of the window to land in a bush nearby where it struck up a chattering tune. I felt myself slipping into a daydream, so I refocused on the knife making and noticed that Mr. Andrews had angled the blade more so as to produce the cutting edge of the blade. A fine, sharp surface became apparent.

"Take a feel of this now," he said, handing me the transformed product.

"Wow, that's sharp! And what a great handle. I love how it fits in my hand." I stood staring at the small, purple knife. "I just can't believe you made this all in one afternoon," I said shaking my head.

"We aren't finished quite yet. Got to touch it up on the buffing wheel. Give it a good shine. Wait 'til you see how that wood polishes. I think you'll like it."

Down the four uneven steps, we struck out across the yard toward the barn. The shadows were growing longer, casting the house in a blanket of shade with only slivers of orange light filtering through. Mr. Andrews paused by a bush covered with tiny, multicolored fruit on its limbs, its trunk protruding from a large, black, plastic pot. I was reminded of a small Christmas tree with little, colored lights.

"You know what this is?" Mr. Andrews asked.

"Looks like a pepper of some kind, but I've never seen one like it," I observed while feeling several of the fruit.

"It's a chili pepper. That's what I make my pepper jelly out of," he said proudly. "See those little ones sprouting at the base? I got more than I know what to do with. I will send you home with some."

Three cats showing interest in our conversation suddenly darted away towards the bushes.

Inside the barn once more, Mr. Andrews showed me his electric buffing wheel on the left hand wall near the drill press. I had not noticed it before, but there were so many tools lying around that I would have had to know what I was looking for to actually find it.

Mr. Andrews flipped on the switch, and the cloth wheel started turning with a quiet humming sound.

Touching what looked like a green piece of chalk to the spinning wheel, he said, "I have always used green polishing compound on my knives. I found that it gets in the metal good and can make the antlers look like ivory in places."

He pressed the handle to the wheel, rotating the

knife in his calloused hands until the entire wood handle had been polished several times over.

"See," he said holding the knife up for me to view the now beautiful, deep purple wood. "See how nice this purple heart wood looks after you polish it?"

Next, he worked on polishing the dull metal of the blade. Quickly the blade took on a totally different appearance with a shiny, reflective sheen. I stood beside Mr. Andrews in awe as I realized what he had accomplished before me. In just one afternoon this 81-year-old man had transformed a piece of a rusty saw blade and two rectangular wood blocks into a beautifully crafted, functional little knife. And suddenly I held my very first handmade knife and the first of many gifts that Mr. Andrews would give me, both material and intangible.

I meticulously scrutinized his work-- the smooth, dark wood so soothing to my hand, the small contoured notch for the index finger, the blade so incredibly shiny.

"Remember to always leave some imperfections," I heard him say while still staring at the knife in my hand. "That's how people will know it's handmade. It's kind of like your signature on the knife."

I looked at Mr. Andrews and then laughed, "I don't think I will ever have to TRY to leave any imperfections!"

In a serious, fatherly tone, he said while taking his cap off his head, "Life is not meant to be perfect, Dr. Curtis. Everyone tries to please everyone else. They think they should try to be perfect. Ain't no man perfect in this world... only Jesus. People should just quit worrying. All anyone can do is just do his best." He paused for a moment while he gazed out across the road at the cows in the distance. "Let's go inside and get your catfish."

I followed Mr. Andrews inside his house. He reached into the refrigerator and grabbed the bag of catfish he had cleaned for me earlier.

"One of these days I will have to show you a good recipe with these things," he said pointing to the catfish meat in the bag.

"Yes sir," I responded. "I would love to try it."

Mrs. Nell entered the kitchen, so sweet and frail, and said quietly, "It was real nice to meet you, Andrew. You are welcome back anytime. We sure would enjoy another visit."

I hugged her small frame and told her that I genuinely appreciated their hospitality. Leading the way out of the house, I walked to my parked truck with Mr. Andrews trailing behind me.

"I like that truck, Dr. Curtis. What year is it?"

Looking at my black Z-71 Chevy truck, I answered, "'04. It's been a good truck."

He began to make small talk about my truck, and I sensed that he was stalling my departure.

Finally, I extended my hand, "Well, Mr. Andrews, it sure was nice to meet you today. I would love to come back."

He caught my hand firmly. "Next time I will start

showing you how to make an antler knife. Takes a little bit longer than that slab handle," he chuckled while nodding toward the knife in my hand. "Come back when you can, Dr. Curtis."

At that, I climbed into my truck, and Mr. Andrews shut the door. As I pulled out of the short, dirt driveway, I peered across the road to the cow pasture. The cows were huddled in the far left corner. Shade had overtaken the field with the setting sun, but the large oak trees beyond were painted with an orange glow from the last half hour's light. I took a right slowly out of the driveway and glanced back just in time to see Mr. Andrews watching me drive off. I was already thinking about my next visit and how incredibly excited I was to learn how to make an antler handle knife. After all, that was the reason I went to Mr. Andrews' house in the first place.

CHAPTER 2:

"Go pick you out a handle you like."

I hurried home from work after closing at noon the following Wednesday. I worked at a veterinary clinic that closed half day every Wednesday, and since my wife would be working all day, I knew those afternoons would be well spent going to visit Mr. Andrews. Once home, I hastily slapped a peanut butter and honey sandwich together and took an apple to eat in the truck, eager as I was to begin my first antler knife lesson. The twenty minute drive west to Carnegie, Georgia, was absolutely gorgeous. Another brilliant October day sprawled ahead of me. The winding, hilly Southwest Georgia terrain made the scenic trip a bonus to the fabulous visits I would have with Mr. Andrews. Making the final turn, I traveled the remaining few miles with mounting excitement. I slowed down to navigate the sharp left curve at my destination and saw Mr. Andrews standing at the bank of his small, green pond. I veered into the side entrance adjacent to the pond and rolled my window down.

"Hey, Dr. Curtis!" he called out with a wave of his hand. "I'm just feeding my catfish."

He was holding the blue coffee container of fish feed. The pond surface rippled with the wakes from the catfish greedily gulping the floating feed pellets.

"Go on and pull up to the house. I'll be right behind you."

I steered my truck slowly up the slight incline to the side of the house, parked, and hopped out onto the grass. The group of cats warily observed my movements, keeping their distance from this stranger. From around the corner of the house, Mr. Andrews appeared with a wide grin spread across his weathered face. He wore a camouflage cap, blue jeans, and a red checkered long sleeve button up shirt with the cuffs rolled halfway up his forearms.

"I brought three antler handles I cut last weekend," I exclaimed proudly. I shook his hand firmly in greeting and then relinquished my antler pieces.

"Hmmm... those are some mighty curved antlers..." I could tell he was trying hard not to offend me. "We might be able to find you a straighter one out in the barn. Follow me."

And so we made the already familiar trip to the work barn. Once inside he pointed to the black and yellow tool box full of antler handles that I had seen on the first day.

"Go pick you out a handle you like."

I tried to hide my excited expression as I hurried over to the toolbox in the center of the barn. My eyes, adjusting to the dim light, danced from one beautiful antler to the next, each of which had been previously cut and ground into a 4-5 inch straight segment of assorted colored antlers. One at the time, I lifted them all out of the box and rolled them around in my hands. Some had the rough ridges at the base of the antler for a more natural look while others had been sanded smooth to give a uniform feel. I favored the natural base look and carefully took stock of my options. Finally, I eyed the one I wanted. Pale yellow with dark brown ridges, the antler curved just so to fit the contour of my right palm. I imagined for a brief moment how the antler would look once completed with a fine, shiny blade protruding from one end.

"I think I found the one I want," I remarked, holding the antler up so Mr. Andrews could inspect.

"I believe that will make a good knife," he said, gently taking the handle from me. Alternating holding in his left then right hand he observed, "This is definitely a right handed handle." His wrinkled, tanned fingers caressed the surface of the ridges. "We will have to touch this handle up a bit, but first let's get going on the blade."

He laid the handle down on a table and picked up a rusty, long rectangular piece of metal. "This is an old planer blade I got from a saw mill years ago. They don't make blades like this anymore. It's some of the best carbon steel I have found."

"So you like carbon steel, not stainless?" I inquired.

"Oh yes sir. There is no comparison. Carbon steel holds an edge so much better. You can clean a whole hog without sharpening it once."

He sat in the chair with the vice in front of him and tightly clamped the metal. After testing the grip by pushing down on the end of the metal, he lifted the hand held grinder from the dirt floor and switched it on. The screaming pitch of the motor prevented further conversation. With the cutting wheel attached to the electric tool, Mr. Andrews began cutting through the resilient steel as yellow-orange sparks flew all about the room. I fearfully stood directly behind him so as not to get hit by any hot bits of metal shavings.

Pausing after several seconds of cutting, he scooped a cup of water from the small cooler beneath the vice.

"Remember, you gotta be careful not to get the metal too hot or it will become brittle and will break easily. It messes with the temper. Always be patient and quench it with water often to cool it down."

He slowly poured water from the red plastic cup evenly and methodically over the steaming metal. Resuming the task of cutting the metal with the shrill din of the machine bouncing off the barn walls, Mr. Andrews morphed the plain strip of metal into an obvious curved knife pattern.

Pausing the high pitched cutting, he remarked more to himself than to me, "About 4 inches... I reckon that's about all the blade any man needs."

Then back to the cutting he went, while I gazed eagerly over his hunched shoulders. I saw his technique, the swift strokes of the wheel, the careful placement in the grooves, the decisive motions of his hands. At last he held up the knife silhouette with a three inch long narrow tang, which would be the piece to fit into the antler handler.

"What do you say we take a break and go eat us some crackers and pepper jelly?"

"Sure sounds good to me," I agreed.

Once inside the house, Mrs. Nell greeted me with a gentle hug and instructed me to sit at the dinner table. Mr. Andrews mixed a concoction of flavored tea and heated the mug in the microwave while Mrs. Nell set out crackers, cream cheese, silverware, colorful flower patterned plates, and Mr. Andrews' signature pepper jelly. Bringing my steaming mug of tea, Mr. Andrews removed his camo cap as he sat down at the table. Quietly, he spread a thin layer of white cream cheese on his multigrain club cracker and topped it off with a dab of pepper jelly. Lifting the crumbly cracker to his mouth, he paused before taking a bite.

"So, Dr. Curtis, what ever made you want to get into knife making?"

I thought for a few seconds before answering.

"Well, I have always enjoyed collecting deer antlers, either from hunting or finding the shed antlers in the woods. I have so many that I began to wonder what I could do with them, like a project or something. I have always loved knives too. I'm not sure collecting is the right word because I don't have that many. For a long time I have specifically wanted an antler knife. So one day I decided to try to make one," I chuckled at my elementary thought process. "But I quickly realized it takes a little more expertise than I have! What about you, Mr. Andrews? How did you get into knife making?"

"Well, I wanted a hobby that didn't cost me much money. The metal and antlers I can get for free. I already had all the tools I needed. Just gotta buy some leather for the sheaths and some brass or nickel silver for the bolsters. That's about it. And I wanted something I could work on when I had time. I could set it down whenever I wanted and resume whenever I wanted. No deadlines. Just go out there and sand on a blade for a few minutes at night or spend an entire rainy day working on one. I'm never bored. And when I'm done, I have something to show for my time. It's important for you to remember to never turn it into a job. Let it be fun. Don't get in a hurry to finish because you will lose interest."

"Don't get in a hurry," I thought. Wow, I felt like we all were in such a hurry to do anything. What's happening to our culture? Efficiency is drilled into us at an early age. If we want to be successful in life, we must be efficient. We must hurry. Time is a wasting, we are taught. Just maybe more people would be happier at their jobs if they could slow down and take a much needed breath from the rapid pace. I repeated the command again in my head: "Don't get in a hurry."

Looking down at my well prepared cracker snack with a sliver of cream cheese and a large heap of pepper jelly, I took a bite. The jelly was just spicy enough to give a jolting kick to my taste buds but left no lingering burn. I sipped my hot tea from the dark green mug, listening to Mr. Andrews talk of his two grandchildren, Mark who lived in Atlanta with his wife Rachel, and Amy who lived in Americus with her husband Grant. Mrs. Nell piped in the conversation periodically showing her admiration of her grandchildren. The conversation shifted towards Mark's and Amy's father, Harold, who lived a quarter mile down the road with his wife Vickie. As the only living child, Harold had taken over the family well drilling business, Andrews Drilling Company, and was seemingly always hard at work. Mr. Andrews was readily available to help with the ever present problem solving aspect of the industry. As I was slowly realizing, Mr. Andrews was knowledgeable about a wide array of topics.

I sat at that table with the recognition of a unique opportunity I had to learn from this elderly man. Over half a century more of experience stared back at me, like an open curriculum awaiting my intellectual probing. I gazed longingly at the wrinkled faces of the couple before me, husband and wife of nearly 60 years. So much of life the two shared together, the smiling picture-worthy moments but also the many struggling, stressful times of raising a family and providing financially.

As if on cue with my ponderings, Mr. Andrews said with a heavy sigh, "Well drilling has been a hard way of life, but it's been good to this family. I can't say we have wanted for much. We just try to make an honest living and have a good name."

Out the window the mid-day autumn sun shone brightly offering enough illumination for us to see comfortably inside the house. I enjoyed the natural lighting and appreciated that the Andrews did too.

Mr. Andrews pushed away from the table, stood up with a low grunt, and pointed out the window behind my chair.

"Let's go see if we can work on that blade some more."

I stood up while Mrs. Nell quickly grabbed my empty plate and tea mug to clear the table. "I can help you with that, Mrs. Nell."

"No," she laughed quietly, her shaky hands continuing their work. "It's quite alright. I got it. Y'all go work on your knife."

We walked out the kitchen door onto the small screen porch, and through the door that always shut with a loud bang. The same group of four cats darted into the shadows of the bushes and watched as we strolled by. A white farm truck honked the horn at Mr. Andrews as it drove by rounding the curve in front of the house. Mr. Andrews held his hand up to acknowledge the driver while continuing on his path to the work barn.

Retrieving the knife blade he had been making, he fit the tang into a black rubber file handle.

"See, Dr. Curtis, now we can hold it easier while we sand the blade."

Back again we strode to the detached kitchen building which housed the two belt sanders. I found it amusing how much walking back and forth was involved in his knife making hobby. I'm sure moving and staying active made his body feel younger.

The temperature outdoors had risen to near 80, but there was still a coolness to the breeze blowing from the north wafting over the hay field. Past the colorful pepper plants and up the creaky, uneven steps we climbed to the sanders. Taking up the work position in the metal chair, Mr. Andrews continued his diligent task of transforming the blade, occasionally pausing to talk to me or to give me detailed directions on how he thought the process should be done.

This was no doubt a form of art. His hand movements had purpose and meaning. Though the process monotonous, it was also therapeutic to watch. Often my mind leaped ahead as I tried to envision the completed product. Those nonverbal intervals of concentrated work allowed my mind to drift, sometimes to a different place than knife making. No matter my thoughts, I felt the rich presence and intertwining spiritual fullness with Mr. Andrews. I could absorb so much information merely by studying the man that he was.

At one point my focus concentrated on his hands-- those stiff, arthritic fingers, the scars coursing across the knuckles, the wrinkled, sun-blotched skin. As if by a magical elixir, the fingers seemed to become more lively as they guided the knife blade against the sanding belt with delicate precision. Mr. Andrews was indeed an artist, his canvas not paper but rough metal. Like the diamond in the rough, he transformed the plain canvas into an eye appealing, multi-functional work of art. Each knife was unique unto itself and could withstand generations of use. Quality was his main ingredient. How much could be learned from this man and his way of life!

Suddenly, Mr. Andrews switched the machine off, and the dull drone of the motor died down. He pushed his glasses with his dusty index finger back higher on the bridge of his nose while studying his blade. His stiff left thumb carefully slid perpendicular to the now angled edge in order to test its sharpness. Those hands were of a working man's. A lifetime of hard work had built an armor of calluses on his palms and fingers.

As he scraped his thumb tip back and forth across the blade edge, he said, "Could be a little sharper for sure, but we will put the finishing edge on later."

He handed over the blade, and I mimicked his thumb motion across the edge to discover that the cutting edge was not too sharp. He intentionally left it dull to reduce the risk of cutting his hand during the remainder of the process. The final step would be to hone the edge to a fine *convex* surface as he would show me later.

I watched my thumb as it went back and forth along the blade's edge. How different these two hands were. Mine so young and smooth compared to his, as if to signal the obvious inexperience of youth. We were both making a living with our hands, but the similarities ended there. My hands were trained for medicine and surgery, to diagnose and treat pets. My job did not require dirt under my fingernails nor a sunburn. Mr. Andrews' hands were trained for strenuous work, getting dirty, being in the outdoor elements, and handling and wrestling heavy machinery. Skinned knuckles and cut fingers were expected. My hands were like a budding flower just beginning to reveal its shape and colors, having never experienced life's major storms. Mr. Andrews' hands reminded me of the brittle leaves still clinging to the pecan tree high above my head. I, like the flower, was so close to the ground, the starting line. He, like the leaves high above, was nearing the finish line. My hands, my life, like the buds were limber and ready to bend with the storms. His hands, his life, like the dying leaves were stiff and brittle. Any storm could potentially dislodge him from the limb and send him down.

For a moment, I imagined his journey down. So graceful. So beautiful. In my mind I saw his gentle release to glide with the wind... over the old white house he had known all his life, with the pond and the garden and the pines and the pastures. The wind would carry him proudly west toward Carnegie where his Baptist church sat waiting. Across the road from the welcoming church, the wind would guide him down to a spot with a pleasant view of a gently sloping field in the distance surrounded by centuries old hardwood trees. And there the leaf would settle.

A gust of wind whistled through the open door snapping me out of my dream, and I could hear the withered pecan leaves above the roof rustle and cling to their tree. It was not yet time to let go…

"Well, Dr. Curtis, let's get started on your bolster. I got a bar of nickel silver in the house."

"Why don't you use brass?"

"I do sometimes, but I've gotten to where I just like that nickel silver. It holds a polished look and stays shiny, doesn't tarnish like brass. But ain't a thing wrong with brass either."

Down the four creaky, bowing steps we went and turned left by the colorful pepper plants in their black pots. A curious half-grown kitten cautiously approached us from the direction of the house, so I knelt down to attempt to coax it my way. It was a male short haired gray tabby cat and peered at me through trusting eyes.

"That one there seems to be getting friendly," Mr. Andrews commented. "See if he'll let you pet him. I will be right back."

Mr. Andrews disappeared into his house while I tried to become acquainted with this cat. Knee in the orange-red dirt, I extended my hand slowly, wiggling my fingers while talking softly to try to convey my trust. Almost within arm's reach, he sat on his haunches and meowed quietly. In his golden eyes I could see that he desired human companionship unlike the other cats in the yard. Out of the corner of my eye, I saw the screen door slowly crack open, and Mr. Andrews poked his grinning face out to view the situation. He eased out the door, and instead of letting it slam loudly, he guided it gently closed so as not to disrupt my efforts.

After a few minutes of watching the stalemate, Mr. Andrews remarked, "I like that little cat. He doesn't act like the rest. I may just have to work with him and try to hand feed him. Bet I can tame him before you come back."

I cautiously rose to my feet in hopes of not frightening our new friend. However, he galloped away soundlessly a short distance then wheeled around as if to have second thoughts. His chance to commit for today was gone, and he seemed to watch us almost regrettably as we walked away toward the barn. A pitiful meow carried in the breeze behind us. Before long that kitten would become our companion.

Once in the barn again, my pupils working overtime, I watched Mr. Andrews place the bar of nickel silver into his open vice grip and tighten it snuggly. Within seconds, the cutting wheel screamed its way through the nickel to release a smaller nearly square shaped section. The drill press was the next stop for the piece of green metal where a hole was punched through the center.

"That's where the tang will go through," he said pointing to the newly formed hole still hot from the metal on metal drilling.

He took a hand file that he had ground down in order to fit inside the hole in the nickel silver. From there he began to manually file the hole for the tang so that the tang would fit snuggly through.

The filing motion was physically taxing, and after a few minutes Mr. Andrews said, "I believe this is where we will stop for the day. We have at least got you started. We have plenty of time to work on this ole knife. I figure you will be coming back soon."

He raised an eyebrow and smiled that dentured grin. He knew I was hooked on this project, and he could take as long as he desired. I would indeed be coming back. My mind was still focused on knife making, but I was not blind to the wonderful relationship we were growing. Mr. Andrews was becoming my buddy, someone I could really talk to.

As we stepped out of the work barn, across the road in front of us lay the peaceful pasture with its Bahia grass and black cows. Behind us and to the left, the sun was ducking behind the tall Loblolly pine stand. To our right sat the house, and farther over the old kitchen house overlooked the small pond at the bottom of the grassy slope. The rectangular garden plot kissed the pond bank which was covered in tall weeds. A dilapidated wood barn with a partially collapsed rust red tin roof silently stared over the garden and pond, but its view was soon to be obscured by nature's tangled growth.

Mr. Andrews paused and peered upward. Nearly directly overhead glowed a crisp crescent moon blanketed by the darkening blue sky. For a few seconds we both stared at this moon, lost in our own dreams. I anticipated him to speak, but his thoughts were never revealed. Without looking back at me, he continued the short trek down the worn foot path to the house.

Kicking his dirty brown boots off just inside the screen door, Mr. Andrews prepared to go rest on his blue couch where the cushion sagged. Through the kitchen and dining room, we walked into the living room and plopped down. Mrs. Nell was already seated in her chair across the room from us. The room was dimly lit, and with dusk approaching, there was a cozy, soothing atmosphere in the room. Mr. Andrews shifted to his left to grasp the drawer handle of the side table, which housed the treasured knife collection. Excitement shot through me as I realized he would show me his beautiful handmade antler knives again.

Pulling one out he said, "See here, this is how I get the blade to sit flush to the bolster. I file a small notch right here, you see that? That way it fits just like a puzzle piece."

Handing the knife to me, he kept his arthritic finger pointing to the notched metal. "Barely detectable," I thought in admiration. Without scrutiny, the knife blade, bolster, and handle appeared to be forged as one single piece, an absolute masterpiece in my eyes. I rolled the dark, smooth antler handle from my right hand to my left and back to my right. It fit in either hand very well. I gave the knife back to its maker in hopes for an exchange. Sure enough, the knife was carefully laid in the open drawer, and another knife was retrieved, this one bound in a light leather sheath. One snap at the top of the sheath held the knife tightly in its grasp. Mr. Andrews quickly popped the snap open and slid the knife out. "Another beautiful creation," I thought, yet this time it was not the knife but the sheath he wished to discuss.

"We will have to make you one like this. I came up with this design because all the other knife sheaths I had bought hung down too low from my belt. Every time I would sit down it would catch real awkward, and I would have to position it with my hand. That's why I put the belt loop lower down so the knife actually rests higher up on your hip." He demonstrated with his left hand on his hip. "I like doing a snap at the top so it doesn't fall out, and it's nothin' to open the snap easily with one hand."

Taking both knife and sheath, I slipped the knife slowly into its case and snapped the leather flap closed. I unclasped my belt and threaded it through the leather loop of the sheath.

Leaning back with disbelief in my voice, I exclaimed, "Wow, I can't even tell I have a knife on my hip! I like that design a lot, Mr. Andrews."

After unfastening the sheath, I handed it back to Mr. Andrews where he replaced it in the drawer. Next out was the mesmerizingly unique knife I had fallen in love with on the first visit, the old mule deer knife. This one for some reason unbeknownst to me did not have a sheath.

"Now that one is probably my favorite I have seen so far. Tell me about that one again."

"This ole thing? Had a friend who found a mule deer shed antler way out in Utah somewhere. Guess it had sat out in the sun drying for a while and began to crack some. That's where all these lines come from. It polished up better than I could have ever imagined. And this blade..." he ran his thumb over the shiny metal. "This blade is some of the best carbon steel I have ever worked with. Just got lucky finding it. Real old. I think I told you I made another knife like it out of the same antler and steel. I used it to clean many a catfish with, Dr. Curtis. Gotta find that thing one of these days. I know it's around this house somewhere."

He paused when he heard his screen door slam shut with a muffled bang. Seconds later the kitchen door opened with a rattle and creak, and I heard heavy footsteps coming our way. A fairly tall, strong framed man with an infectious, natural smile poked his head in through the doorway. He beamed down at me while extending his hand.

"Harold Andrews," I heard him say as I reached for his hand in a rising motion.

I introduced myself and felt my mouth crease upward in a wide smile like his.

"Daddy told me a lot about you. I just had to drop by and say hey."

We stood talking for a few minutes before he said, "Well, Doc, it sure was nice to meet you. I guess I better head on to the house." He turned to leave but wheeled back around. "Oh, Daddy, we were working over there off 41 and ran into a problem about 315 feet down..."

The well driller's lingo went over my head and out the door, but I did notice that Mr. Andrews offered his son a confident solution to the problem. Mr. Andrews seemed to be a wise man without flaunting. He was a man who knew he was right, but in no way was arrogance a part of his demeanor. As I looked at Mr. Andrews, a quote flashed through my mind: "He who knows and knows that he knows is wise. Follow him." I was determined to learn from this humble man and absorb all that I could from him.

Harold said his goodbyes again and quickly departed.

Looking at my watch, I realized that it was getting late and time for me to go too.

"My wife should be home soon, so I better hit the road. I really enjoyed coming over here today, y'all."

"Won't you stay for supper with us?" sweet Mrs. Nell inquired graciously.

"Oh I would love to but maybe another night soon." I responded regretfully.

"I'll walk you out, Dr. Curtis," Mr. Andrews said pushing up off the low couch. "Let me cut you some of that pecan pie to take with you. You like pecan pie?"

"Yes sir, I love it."

"Good, I will cut you a piece for your wife too."

Carefully cradling my dessert, I went out the kitchen and through the screen door, down the concrete steps, and headed for my truck parked by the side of the house near the old muscadine vine. Mr. Andrews followed me and opened my truck door.

We made small talk for a few minutes and then he said, "Well, come back when you can, Dr. Curtis."

CHAPTER 3:

"It's your knife now."

"**A**lright, Dr. Curtis, it's time for the spacers now. Don't ask me why, but I always do red first, then white, then black. I guess I just like the way it looks."

Nearly a month had passed since my first visit, and I had already lost count of the number of knife sessions we had had together since his birthday. The process to make an antler knife proved indeed more tedious than the simple slab handle knife we made on day one. After countless hours of grinding, sanding, drilling, filing, and dremeling, we were nearing the completion of my first handmade deer antler knife. Fashioning the colored spacers between the handle and bolster was the last step before sealing the knife tang into the handle with epoxy. Now this thing looked like a knife!

Mr. Andrews cracked open a tube of epoxy and squeezed the translucent, viscous fluid into the previously drilled hole in the end of the antler. He slowly pushed the tang equipped with the three colored spacers and the nickel silver bolster into the handle slot while epoxy oozed out, sliding down the antler in a sticky mess. He held the knife up close to his face like looking down a gun barrel to be sure the blade was in line with the handle and perpendicular to the bolster. The epoxy would require several minutes to harden, so Mr. Andrews held the blade in place to ensure no misalignment.

Staring out the large, open doorway, Mr. Andrews said, "When my great grandfather settled around these parts, there were still quite a few Indians roaming around these woods. Hard to believe, huh? Wasn't all that long ago really. Those folks back then had to be careful. It was after the Trail of Tears. Guess the government didn't get all the Indians out, and those who were left were pretty upset with the white man. Can't say I blame them."

"What Indian tribe was here?"

"The Creeks at that time. We got all kinds of artifacts around here. I've found quite a few arrowheads just drilling wells."

I was continually amazed at Mr. Andrews' knowledge and accurate details on such a wide range of topics. I am not sure I ever heard him say, "I don't know." Satisfied that the epoxy had hardened sufficiently to ensure the blade not to shift, he carefully wrapped the knife in a dirty, red cloth before gently clamping it in the vice.

"Let's give it a good hour to set and dry. Come see how much my catfish have grown."

The day was fairly warm for November and mostly cloudy, but the sun would peek through the white cloud cover occasionally. A soft breeze rattled the brown, dried pecan leaves, but they still clung to the tree. Most of the leaves were already scattered on the ground and crunched beneath our shoes. A few withered leaves fluttered down in front of our path as we made our way toward the pond. Tidbit, the kitten that Mr. Andrews had tamed and subsequently named, met us halfway to the pond, meowed loudly, then brushed his arched back against our legs. I knelt down to scratch behind his ears, and his eyes closed in a most soothing expression while his lips curled to resemble a smile. The low purr was loud enough to be heard several feet away, his way of informing us of his pleasure.

"I like that cat," Mr. Andrews said with a humorous grin. "He's a bad joker!"

There was a way that he drew out the "a" sound in "bad" that tickled me, like the way one mimics a sheep. Bent over at the waist, Mr. Andrews slowly reached down to pat Tidbit's head.

"Come on, buddy," he said kindly to his little friend, and off we went to the pond.

The blue coffee container that held the fish feed was already by the pond beside two metal folding chairs. I laughed to myself at the sight of the second chair, which was now a fixture at the pond's bank. The two chairs sat side by side looking out over the water. By my third visit, Mr. Andrews had placed a chair beside his for me to sit in, and that's where it stayed.

We both took a seat at the water's edge. Tidbit stood proudly beside Mr. Andrews, his tail flicking and ears erect while staring at the pond. Mr. Andrews offered me a handful of the brown fish pellets, but I waited on him to throw some in before I did. Immediately, the surface of the pond erupted into a splashing frenzy as catfish nearly catapulted out of the water trying to feast on the pellets. I'm not sure if Tidbit was tortured or amused, but he paced back and forth along the edge of the grassy bank jerking his head side to side at each new splash. The sun appeared from behind the non-menacing clouds for a moment, and I could see the flashes of metallic white as the smooth catfish skin would reflect the light and then vanish.

"Did you see the size of that one? I'm telling you these fish get bigger by the week. Got some good eatin' size in here," he remarked.

I watched as the floating feed disappeared into the gluttonous mouths. Now an occasional swirl would appear where a morsel had been missed. The ripples on the water became less frequent allowing the reflection of the oaks on the far bank to reappear. We sat talking and staring at the clear, green pond, every once in a while spotting a fish cruising just below the surface. Tidbit had given up hope of catching a fish, sitting contently next to Mr. Andrews.

"Dr. Curtis, what do you say we go check on your knife? I reckon we should start the sheath too."

On the way back up the slope to the work barn, he detoured to retrieve a rectangular sheet of leather from the house. He showed me the light brown leather rubbing it between his fingers.

"This is the kind of leather you want for your knives. You gotta be careful because a lot of leather out there will rust a knife."

"What kind of leather is that?" I inquired.

"100% vegetable tanned cow hide. Got this piece from Tandy Leather. Ever heard of them?"

"No sir," I replied.

"Sometimes I get it from Jantz. I have a catalogue you can take with you."

We went into the barn and released the knife from the vice. Mr. Andrews was satisfied with the blade set after inspecting by looking down the spine as he had done before. Dipping the leather in his small cooler of water in order to make the leather pliable, he positioned the knife in the center of the leather and folded it over the knife. He pressed down firmly to allow the saturated leather to contour to the knife's shape.

Handing me the freshly folded leather, he said, "Time to go finish your knife."

We ended up on the cracked, wooden stairs outside the old kitchen house. Sitting on the second step, he opened up a small black folding knife he kept in his pants pocket and began to whittle the colored spacers flush with the handle. After fifteen minutes he climbed the remaining two steps into the kitchen house and flipped on the one inch sanding belt. I realized with excitement that my knife was nearing completion. After sanding for a while, Mr. Andrews leaned back in his chair to examine his work. "Now I'm going to buff this thing out and get it smooth and shiny."

The buffing wheel, located in the work barn, looked like a motor from 100 years ago. Applying green polishing compound to the wheel, he delicately touched all components of the knife to the spinning fabric wheel. Suddenly, the transformation was complete. There before me was the knife I knew I would keep and love forever. Not only a keepsake to be handed down to a future generation, but also one that would play a functional role in my life. This was my knife, one of a kind. No other knife on earth was like it. One day this beautiful knife would tell a story, one that I would help create.

"Here you go, Dr. Curtis. Tell me what you think. It's your knife now. A lot of people just keep a knife like this in a drawer, maybe pull it out once in a while and look at it, but I sure hope you use it."

I heard the words distantly tumble out of my mouth, my eyes fixated on the gift. "I absolutely love it..." I trailed off, deep in thought. I ran my thumb along the smooth surface of the blade and then across the ivory like area of the antler that he had polished so finely.

"Remember, always leave some imperfections. That's how people will know it's handmade."

His words echoed in my mind. I knew I would never forget the way he said that.

"'Bout time we take a break. How 'bout some crackers and pepper jelly?"

"Yes sir, that sounds great to me."

Carrying my knife so proudly, I light-footedly followed Mr. Andrews back to his house. Mrs. Nell was in the kitchen. Mr. Andrews reached in the fridge and got out the cream cheese and jelly.

"Grab that box of crackers, and I will meet you at the table. I'm going to heat you up some tea."

The colorful flower plates were set on the table with some silverware. Mrs. Nell took a seat to join me in the dining room, and after a few minutes the microwave dinged. In came Mr. Andrews with the hot, aromatic tea in a dark blue mug in one hand and the cream cheese and jelly cradled in the other arm. The three of us snacked and talked. The conversation, like all the times before, drifted toward Amy and Mark, their two beloved grandchildren. They each took turns filling me in on the latest updates in the family.

Mr. Andrews, holding his empty blue tea mug in his wrinkled, stiff hands, looked at me and said, "Dr. Curtis, there is something I want to show you. Let's go in there and sit on the couch a bit."

Once on the soft couch, Mr. Andrews leaned over the armrest and lifted up a magazine that was resting on the side table.

"You see, about twelve years ago I went to the GAGwP (Georgia Association of Groundwater Professionals) annual auction and decided to give one of my antler knives to the executive director. I took two there to let him pick his favorite. When the auction started, I told Harold to run to the truck and grab the other knife. I figured it would bring $100 or so. It actually went for $500."

"Wow!" I exclaimed in an admiring tone. "The crowd must have really loved your knife." He nodded and grinned.

"Since then it seems to be getting more popular every year. Last year it went for $3500."

"$3500!" I interrupted, nearly jumping off the couch. "I was already proud to have this knife you made me, but now I *know* I have something special!"

His smile widened as he opened the magazine to an article called "Mr. Andrews' Knives" dated November 2011. Sure enough, right there in blue type to contrast the rest of the black font was the amount $3500. The article described the knives and how popular they have been.

I read aloud the last two sentences of the final paragraph: "The association will forever be indebted to Mr. Andrews for his generous contributions to GAGwP. These knives are a real collector's item, and all the owners agree that they are truly priceless!" I slowly set the magazine down on the coffee table in front of me and turned to face Mr. Andrews. "You should really be proud of this, Mr. Andrews."

"Nothin' to be proud of, Dr. Curtis. Just an old hobby that turned into something that people like."

"I feel like I should pay you something for this knife," I said humbly.

He dismissed my comment with a waving hand gesture and looked me in the eyes as he replied, "You already have, Dr. Curtis. You already have."

I thought about what he said for a moment, bewildered. The true meaning escaped me at the moment. It wasn't until years later that I realized what he was referring to... my time.

We spent the next hour talking and poring over his astonishing knife collection. I, of course, got the chance to hold my favorite knife of his, the magnificently polished mule deer knife with the extremely old steel blade.

Glancing at my watch I reported, "I should probably get on back to the house."

Mr. Andrews rose off the couch and said, "Next time we will finish your sheath. And if you have time I might make you some shrimp creole."

"I would love that," I sincerely replied. "I'm looking forward to it."

He followed me out the slamming screen door, past the group of cats huddled together, and to my parked truck at the side of the white house by the muscadine vine. We talked at the truck door for several minutes.

"I really do appreciate this knife you made me."

He grinned with a slight nod of his head. "Come back when you can, Dr. Curtis."

CHAPTER 4:

"Andrew Carnegie... the billionaire."

The day was seasonably cool for the first week of December. Between work and Thanksgiving Holiday I hadn't been able to visit Mr. Andrews for nearly two weeks, and I was chomping at the bit to finish my leather knife sheath. My truck came to rest in my usual parking spot by the house. I stepped out of my truck into the glary sunshine. A fairly stiff, cold wind brushed across my face and rattled the few remaining crisp pecan leaves above me. Only a few clusters of leaves now hung on to the branches. They seemed to have security in numbers. Despite the wind, the leaves still clung stubbornly to their tree.

"Hey, Dr. Curtis!"

I transferred my gaze from the tree branches above to the work barn where I had heard the familiar greeting.

"Hey, Mr. Andrews, how you doing?"

He was dressed in heavily stained blue jeans, red flannel shirt with a tan jacket unzipped, and a blue and white cap.

"Just out here working on a knife. Come on, let's go inside and work on your sheath."

Tidbit came galloping up to me with a long drawn-out meow and brushed his arched body against my shin. I bent over to scratch his head and heard Mr. Andrews say, "That's a bad joker right there. He rules the roost now."

We walked up the steps into the warm house where Mrs. Nell greeted me happily in the dining room. Mr. Andrews led me to the couch and picked up the leather that we had begun to shape the previous visit.

"The next step is to go ahead and put the belt loop on."

With a handheld leather punching tool, he made three overlapping holes near what would be the opening of the sheath. He then cut with his small black pocket knife a strip of leather about a half inch wide and four inches long, the smell of leather permeating the room. Threading one end of the leather strip through the hole he had punched, he secured it with a round, silver rivet at each end of the strip. And so the belt loop was on! He then cut out a curved strip of leather to match the curve of the knife blade and cut the sheath with this same curved line. He folded the sheath in half and positioned the curved strip of leather in between and applied glue to hold the strip in place.

"Time to go put this in the vice grip and wait for it to dry. I want to show you the blade I have started to work on too."

Out the house and across the yard we walked, crunching the brown, dried pecan leaves that blanketed the ground beneath our shoes. Mr. Andrews wrapped the sheath in a denim cloth and placed it in his vice to hold while the glue dried. Beside the vice lay a rusty planer blade with a knife pattern carved out of one end.

"You like the shape of this blade?" he asked.

"Yes sir, I sure do. Who's that going to be for?"

"Still want to make your dad and father-in-law knives?" he inquired with a wink.

"Yes sir... but... I mean... you don't have to..."

"I want to," he interjected. "I figure if we both work on them, we can finish by Christmas."

"There's no rush, Mr. Andrews, really. I can give them an IOU at Christmas and give them the knives whenever we finish." He grinned as he fumbled through the black and yellow toolbox that housed the antler handles.

"What size hands do they have?" he wondered aloud.

"My father-in-law has really big hands. My dad's hand is about the size of mine." I held my hand out palm up, fingers spread apart. Chuckling to himself he extracted a wonderfully colored straight antler piece larger in diameter than my knife's handle.

"This ought to fit a great big ole hand. What you think?"

"I think that's just right, Mr. Andrews."

"Ok, how 'bout this one for your dad?" With his other hand he showed me a smooth, slightly curved antler base.

"I love them both, but I don't want you to feel like you have to do this." I was thinking about his auction knife selling for $3500.

"I wouldn't do it if I didn't want to," he said in a more serious tone. "What do you say we go catch some fish?"

Down the hill we trod with Tidbit joining us as we passed by the house. We snagged two fishing poles from the kitchen house on the way to the pond. The two metal chairs, side by side, awaited our arrival. Tidbit raced us down to the bank and twitched his tail excitedly. He loved this catfish game. Scattering a handful of fish feed onto the pond's rippled surface, we waited a few seconds as the dozens of concentric circles grew larger. Then the first fish appeared, followed by another, then too many at once to count.

"This colder weather hasn't stopped these catfish from biting," he remarked.

I threaded a plump earthworm on my hook and made a cast. Mr. Andrews watched my cork sit idly on the surface. After a few minutes of no nibbles, he instructed me to reel in my line. Grabbing my cork he slid it up the line away from the hook to increase the depth of my hook.

"Now try it. Cast over there. Yeah, right there."

I followed the direction of his outstretched arm. Thirty seconds later my cork began a steady movement away from me, out to the middle of the pond.

"Got one!" I yelled, setting the hook. I fought the catfish to the bank where Mr. Andrews insisted on removing the hook from the writhing fish's mouth.

"Want to keep any?" he asked me.

"No thanks. You can let him go. I'm looking forward to that shrimp creole you promised me," I said with a laugh.

"I wasn't sure if you were going to take me up on my offer tonight or not," he laughed back at me.

Tidbit looked up at us and meowed as if to offer his input on the matter. The catfish hit the water with a splash and would live to fight another day.

"That one might not be so lucky next time. He could end up in my catfish stew."

"When are you going to make that stew for me, Mr. Andrews?"

"Waiting on the right time. Gotta do it for a special occasion," he said with humor in his speech.

We continued to fish and talk, catching several more catfish that we subsequently released.

"I sure could use a snack," he said touching his hand to his belly.

"You read my mind. I could stand some crackers and pepper jelly," I said through a hungry smile.

On the way inside we stopped by the work barn to retrieve my sheath, which had dried. Once inside I automatically walked to my chair at the dinner table with my back to the window as Mr. Andrews brought our tea and snacks. Mrs. Nell joined us as we chat and laughed. While Mrs. Nell cleared the table after finishing eating, Mr. Andrews and I went into the living room and sat on the couch. He put two rivets in place to anchor the leather strip we had just glued and secured a snap at the opening of the sheath to allow the knife to slide in and out. Then, wielding an ice pick, Mr. Andrews began the meticulous task of punching tiny consecutive holes along the folded edge of the sheath.

"A lot of times I will do this hole punching while I watch TV. It takes a little while, but once you do it a few times, you can about do it in your sleep."

Out the window I heard the wind gust through the overgrown shrubs.

"Must have a cold front coming," I said.

"They say it's supposed to get close to freezing tonight," he responded. "It's a good night for some shrimp creole."

When the last hole was punched, Mr. Andrews picked up a role of yellow waxed string and attached it to a straight sewing needle. He wove the string in and out through the holes until he had gone down and back the length of the folded edge of the sheath. I watched his smooth, methodical motions, focusing on his stiff hands. They were surprisingly nimble despite the nagging arthritis. His finger movements were quick and efficient but in an unhurried manner. When the needle found its way through the final hole, he tied a square knot and put a dab of epoxy on the knot.

Out to the sanding belt we went to put the finishing touch on the sheath. He sanded the rough edges and smoothed out the curve.

After about five minutes of sanding, he cut the sander's motor off with a sigh and said, "That should do it. Where's your knife?"

"In my truck," I responded as I made my way to get it.

I brought the knife back and handed it over to Mr. Andrews who sat patiently waiting. He unfastened the snap and carefully slid my knife into its sheath.

"Fits just right, Dr. Curtis. Why don't you try her on?"

I excitedly grasped the sheath with the knife secured inside and threaded the leather onto my belt. Amazingly, I did not feel the knife handle poke into my side or leg when I sat in the chair. Mr. Andrews was correct. He had discovered a sheath design that was indeed comfortable to wear.

"I'm going to want to wear this knife around everywhere," I happily exclaimed.

"I sure hope you do. Maybe you won't stick it in a drawer and forget about it!"

"No sir, I won't be forgetting about this special knife."

He nodded approvingly. "We got some time to kill

before I start on supper. Let's work on those Christmas knives."

The cold NW wind whipped across our bodies. Dry brown leaves tumbled on the ground past our feet. Low, patchy clouds zoomed by overhead like they were trying to hurry to the next town. The cows in the pasture across the road were lying down huddled in a group. Once we were inside the work barn, the biting wind could not reach us. The temperature was cool but pleasant without the wind chill. Mr. Andrews reached for a rusty planer blade in one of the dark corners of the barn.

"That blade I started cutting on earlier today will be your father-in-law's knife. I'm going to cut out a pattern for your dad's knife now. You got a grinder at home, don't you?"

"Yes sir, I just bought one a week ago. Haven't even used it yet."

"I figure you can work on one 'til next time, and I will work on the other. Then we will swap. I think we can get them done by Christmas if you want to... but don't make a job out of it. Only work on it when you have time and want to."

I believe he knew that he would shoulder the bulk of this project's weight, but he wanted me to begin my unsupervised lessons.

"That's mighty generous of you, Mr. Andrews, but... um..."

"But what? Look I wouldn't do it if I didn't want to.

It gives this old man something to do," he laughed.

I laughed too, but I felt as though my expression revealed my thought. Mr. Andrews had plenty in his life to keep him busy. Generosity was in his makeup. He flipped on the screaming, deafening grinder and began chewing through the hot, rusty metal. Just as the blade turned blue, the cutting was paused and water was lightly poured over the hot surface to produce a sizzling layer of bubbles.

"I'm going to curve this tip up slightly at the end, see?"

I watched as the tip took on the shape he described. Every blade he made was indeed unique. No pattern was used. It was all in his mind. I marveled at his artistic eye for this trade. The grinder's wail stopped again.

"You wouldn't know it now, but Carnegie used to be a thriving little town."

"Your address is Cuthbert, right?" I asked.

"Yes. Carnegie became unincorporated in '95. The town center is just a mile down this road," he pointed west. "In the 1890s a post office was built down there, but they called it Grubb. Guess they didn't like the name because about ten years later in 1903, it was changed to Carnegie." He took his glasses off, wiped them on his flannel shirt, then put them back on his face. "Named after Andrew Carnegie... the billionaire. He was born in the 1800s and made his money in the steel industry here in the US. He donated a heap of money in his lifetime."

"Steel, huh?" my curiosity peaked. "You think you've come across any of his steel for your knives?"

He looked at me and winked. "You never know. I have a mighty old piece of steel in that house," he said evasively.

"Is that the steel that you used for your two mule deer knives?"

"Yes, that's the steel." He answered, his smile widening.

I was completely fascinated by the thought. Each piece of metal held a story before Mr. Andrews even acquired it, a past that would remain a mystery to us. I realized that both of us were peering out across the road at the cows down the hill in the pasture. Mr. Andrews was pondering something too. I wondered if by chance we were thinking similar thoughts.

Again, the handheld grinder whined intensely as it cut into the hot metal. A large chunk of the metal fell away to the dirt floor, and there before me lay an unmistakable knife silhouette. One day soon I would present that to my dad as a special gift.

"Alright, we got us a starting point now. Why don't you take the one for your father in law, and I will work on your dad's?"

We walked out in the yard. The wind still blew cold and whistled in the branches above our heads. Quickly we made our way into the warm house and stopped in the kitchen.

"Now time for some shrimp creole!" He declared "Why don't you go in there and sit on the couch and visit with Nell. I'll get this supper fixed up."

I said, "Just let me know if I can do anything to help." He dismissed my offer with a subtle head shake and motion of his hand. I found Mrs. Nell peacefully sitting in her chair, a white, knit blanket draped over her thin legs. "Hey, Mrs. Nell, Mr. Andrews told us to visit while he cooks."

"Oh, Edwin loves to cook. He's good at it too. I used to cook more than I do now, but I just haven't been feeling good lately. This diabetes is giving me a fit. Edwin has always been a good husband to me. I feel like I have been sick most of our marriage, but he always has the best attitude." She paused a few seconds and with a wistful expression said, "I grew up right down there on the other side of the creek, but I didn't know Edwin for a long time. The first time I met him I thought to myself, 'I'm going to marry that boy someday'." The wrinkles in her face drew taut as she gave a reminiscing smile. In the kitchen the sound of a knife on a cutting board could be heard. "And he's been the best friend any woman could ask for."

"What a powerful relationship," I thought. Our relaxing chat continued and then drifted to her son, Harold, and then to Amy and Mark. I watched her eyes dart around the room, recalling sweet memories of her family. Her delicate, wrinkled hands were neatly placed in her blanketed lap. A delicious aroma from the kitchen wafted into the room, so I inhaled slowly, deeply.

"You notice that pretty little brick church up the road you pass by?" Mrs. Nell asked softy. "My brother helped build that. Soon after, he was killed in a car accident. He was the first one to be buried in that cemetery. Come to think of it, I need to go put new flowers on his grave."

"I would like to go see his grave sometime," I said sincerely.

"There aren't too many young people now days who care about stuff like that. I try to keep flowers on the graves of all my family and friends."

"Alright, Dr. Curtis!" echoed a voice from the kitchen. "I sure hope you like my shrimp creole. May not be as good as my catfish stew, though, but still a darn good recipe."

I patiently helped Mrs. Nell to her feet, standing up ever so slowly, and walked with her to the dining table. Mr. Andrews was already serving my bowl.

"Sit down. I will bring the food."

I obeyed as Mrs. Nell and I took our seats. Before sitting, Mr. Andrews removed his blue and white cap and hooked it on the back of his chair.

He bowed his head and prayed, "Our gracious Father, thank you for our many blessings, for our friends, and the good times we share. Help us to serve you the best we can in a humble and honorable way. We ask that you bless this food in Jesus Christ's name. Amen."

"Amen." Mrs. Nell and I responded quietly in unison.

"Dr. Curtis, now you feel free to get you a second helping," Mr. Andrews said.

The meal was incredibly tasty and satisfying, topped off with a cold glass of sweet tea. Pound cake that Mrs. Nell baked the day before was served for dessert. Moist and rich, the cake encouraged me to refill my glass of tea.

"I sure appreciate the meal, Mr. Andrews."

"I'm going to send you some home to give to your wife. Let me know how she likes it."

I hugged Mrs. Nell as I stood to leave. Mr. Andrews dipped me a serving to take home, pouring the creole in an empty Cool Whip container. Stepping out into the dark, cold air, I smiled as I thought about my knife. My fingers caressed the smooth leather sheath attached to my right hip. My left hand clung to the piece of metal that would be my father in law's blade.

"Mr. Andrews, you don't know how much I appreciate your help," I said grasping his toughened hand firmly in a departing handshake.

"I enjoy it, Dr. Curtis. Come back when you can."

I opened my truck door and climbed in. Handing me the shrimp creole, Mr. Andrews opened his mouth as if to speak, but instead he grinned widely and gently shut my door. It would be many visits later before I learned what he had wanted to say to me then.

CHAPTER 5:

"Something's got a hold of Tidbit's tail."

I felt my phone vibrating in my hip pocket while I finished treating an abscess on the side of an English Pointer hunting dog. I glanced at the wall clock: 11:16. It was Wednesday, January 2, 2013, and I would be off work at noon. After a few minutes I peeked at my phone screen and saw a missed call and voicemail from Mr. Andrews. Bringing the phone to my ear, I listened to the recording.

"Dr. Curtis, something's got a hold of Tidbit's tail. Pulled the skin clean off. Just wanted to see if you could bring some medicine when you come this afternoon."

Not knowing the extent of the injury, I decided to be prepared. I drew up an injectable sedative plus antibiotic and anti-inflammatory shots. As my half work day came to a close, I hurried home to change clothes and eat a sandwich. Turning my truck west, I took the pleasant drive towards Carnegie. I wheeled into the red dirt driveway and noticed Mr. Andrews sitting on his back steps petting Tidbit. Immediately I recognized the bright red and white streaked tail as an obvious degloving wound, like someone had stripped the whole skin and fur off as in skinning an animal.

"Ouch!" I grimaced, stepping out of my parked truck. "Poor Tidbit. That is some tail wound."

"Yes sir, Dr. Curtis, I knew he needed some help from you."

"We aren't going to be able to save that tail. He will have to be content as a bobtailed cat from now on."

It was an unseasonably warm day for January, even in South Georgia. The air was calm and humid, and a few patchy clouds drifted high above. The sun shone directly and hot on my face. A few solitary, crisp, brown pecan leaves hung randomly in the tree over me, clinging ever so vulnerably to their limbs. Even a subtle breeze threatened their lofty existence. How did these few leaves hang on so long through wind and storms? There they were, the proud and stubborn few to greet the new year. I felt as though they had beaten great odds prolonging their destined flight to the ground.

My eyes came down to land on Tidbit's tail once more. "Alright, Mr. Andrews, I'm going to have to give a shot of sedation. Once he's good and asleep, I will amputate all but about an inch of his tail."

Insisting on helping, Mr. Andrews snagged Tidbit's scruff tightly as I plunged the injection needle deep into the hamstring muscle. Tidbit let out a surprised meow, scurried out of Mr. Andrews' lap, and peered back at us with insulted, wide eyes. Shortly after, he wobbled as if drunk and then reluctantly squatted down on the lawn.

His nose slowly touched the grass and his tongue flicked involuntarily out of his mouth.

Picking up Tidbit's limp body, I set him on a towel on the floor of the screened porch and administered two more injections, one an antibiotic, the other an anti-inflammatory. Beads of sweat began to form on my scalp as I worked from a crouched position on the humid porch. I tightened a tourniquet around the base of the tail and laid out my sterile drape and surgical pack. Donning my surgical gloves and wielding a scalpel blade in my right hand, I began my incision about an inch from the tourniquet. The scalpel blade worked its way in a circumferential pattern, diving deeper towards the intervertebral joint space. I delicately maneuvered the blade into the joint space and sliced through the binding ligaments with a quick stroke. The injured tail slipped away and landed with a soft thud on the towel. After tying off the arteries, I sutured the skin closed over the tail stump and applied a compression bandage.

"Ok, that should fix him up. He looks more like a bobcat now, doesn't he?"

"He's a bad joker!" Mr. Andrews chuckled in his drawn out manner.

"Let's let him wake up out here on the porch. It's warm and I will wrap this towel around him. We can check on him in a few minutes," I suggested.

"You got room for some pepper jelly and crackers?"

"Yes sir, I sure do!" I answered.

Pushing the old, slightly offset kitchen door open, we stepped inside and went to the living room to greet Mrs. Nell. I spoke to her as Mr. Andrews retrieved the pepper jelly, and we sat down at our respective places at the dining table.

"So what did your Dad and father-in-law think of their knives?" Mr. Andrews asked curiously, though knowing the answer.

This was my first visit since the Christmas holidays. Surprisingly to me we had completed both knives complemented with smooth leather sheaths in time for Christmas. Although Mr. Andrews did the majority of the work, I was proud of the small contribution that I made to each.

"They absolutely loved them, Mr. Andrews. And they both said to tell you thank you. They will keep those knives the rest of their lives."

Mr. Andrews' look of satisfaction on his face made me smile.

"I've been thinking, Mr. Andrews, about the next knife I would like to make. I would like to make one out of elk antler. You got any lying around?"

I anticipated a "no," but to my delight he said, "I got two whole elk antlers out there in the barn. Each antler has a heap of handles in it."

He crunched his dentures into another jelly topped club cracker and chewed slowly. He sipped his tea and looked down at the table in thought.

"Come on. I'll show you what I got."

Leaving the snack ingredients on the table, we stepped out the kitchen door onto the screen porch. Tidbit was still snoozing on the towel with an occasional twitch of his whiskers. The sun had made this January day even hotter than before. We followed the heavily trodden foot path to the work barn, and I gazed at the cows directly across the road from us, not far from where we stood. They looked at us with unconcerned, lazy eyes more interested in their cud chewing. One smaller black cow had her head stuck through the strands of barbed wire to munch on the grass on our side of the fence.

"Guess the grass is greener on the other side," joked Mr. Andrews.

Several buzzards circled slowly over the pasture, gaining altitude with each passing loop. Inside the barn I found Mr. Andrews rummaging in a tin tub, which had been obscured from view by one of his work tables. Not only were there two well colored elk antlers, but also there lay a small caribou rack. My heart thumped more palpably as I ran my fingers along the smooth tine of one of the elk antlers. This would be my next knife. What was the story of this antler? Where did it come from? Where did this elk travel? What did this elk see? And when? Curiosity burst through my mind and out my open mouth.

"Where did you get this beautiful elk antler?"

As if to understand my seemingly endless stream of thoughts he replied with a slight sigh of regret, "Got it from a guy who found this shed antler somewhere out in Montana. Wish I knew the story more. Isn't it funny how deer can cast off their antlers every year and grow new ones? I have made knives out of freshly shed antlers and thought how ironic it was that the buck would still be alive roaming the woods while I had a knife with a piece of the buck himself."

We both stared out the open barn door to the sunlit pasture beyond, lost in our own thoughts. Finally breaking the silence, Mr. Andrews refocused on our mission of selecting an elk handle.

"You like that tine?"

He saw my hand wrapped around a slightly curved, smooth, striped tine that fit nicely in my palm. "The right diameter and length," I thought.

He confirmed my assumption saying, "Oh, yes sir, that ought to make you a fine knife. Bring it here, and I will cut it for you."

Grasping a rusty hacksaw in his stiff left hand and pinning the antler against the table with his right, he sawed effortlessly with quick, rhythmic strokes back and forth. The saw teeth cut neatly through the antler, and the tine fell away to the dirt floor. He picked up the piece and wiped the dirt off on his jeans, inspecting the newly discovered knife handle.

"Yes sir," he reiterated, "that is going to be a fine knife indeed."

Next, he combed through a stack of old, brown

planer blades and handed me one. "Good piece of carbon steel right here," he informed me. I studied the blade and tine in excited wonder trying to imagine the completed product.

"What do you say we go feed the catfish?" he suggested, pointing in the direction of the pond.

On the way to the pond, I detoured to my truck and placed my new knife essentials inside. I looked back at a smiling Mr. Andrews who seemed fully aware of my eagerness to produce my first solo knife. He was turning the helm over to me I knew. I felt the intangible shift. He was still the master, and I was the ambitious pupil. I was taking control of the steering wheel, but he would remain in the co-pilot's seat, right beside me.

Light-footedly, I strolled back to Mr. Andrews, and we trekked the short decline to the pond. The blue Maxwell House container with the fish feed was already placed by the metal chairs at the water's edge. I chuckled to myself thinking of Mr. Andrews filling the container earlier that morning and carrying it down to the pond. Feeding the fish had become as consistent and sure a routine in our visits as our pepper jelly snack time or our couch sitting knife collection perusal and discussions. The water seemed to produce a therapeutic impression in our minds and deeper in our spirits. I could feel it and could sense that Mr. Andrews felt it too. At times, sitting side by side, we would not even speak a word for minutes on end. The laryngeal silence was far from awkward, however. In fact, I felt a strong, determined inner strength pulling me towards Mr. Andrews' emotions. In these moments I could undistractedly connect with a man, a friend, I knew as wise, devoted, selfless, generous, caring, and above all, humble. He was the epitome of a role model. It's a shame the world could not know Mr. Andrews.

On this hot, still day the sun's light pierced the dark water's surface to form a near perfect reflective medium to view the dense wall of oaks hovering over one bank silhouetted by the blue sky above. So clear was the image that Mr. Andrews and I stood side by side mesmerized by the beauty before us. Although I could not read his thoughts, I experienced an emotional connection with him as we peered at the same soul-stimulating scene. At last Mr. Andrews twisted off the container's lid to grab a fistful of pellets. Into the water he scattered the feed, and the swirls began to appear, disrupting our picture-still reflective landscape.

"I've told you about my catfish stew," Mr. Andrews said without diverting his eyes from the pond. "It's one of my favorite dishes. I used to joke with one of my friends about it. We call it the Almost Famous Catfish Stew." He paused to let out a laugh. "It's so good it's on the verge of being famous but not quite famous yet. Maybe with a little more time and another tweak or two, it will become famous. Until then it will be the Almost Famous Catfish Stew!" He laughed harder at this comment, revealing the obvious joking tone.

I joined in the laughter and said, "I hate to admit this, but I have never had catfish stew of any kind."

"I will spoil you with this one then. It's the best one out there. It's simple but mighty good."

"When will you make it for me?" I asked earnestly.

"When the time is right, Dr. Curtis. You see, that's the thing about the Almost Famous Catfish Stew. It's kinda like the unwritten rule. You can only make it for a special occasion." He got tickled as he explained it to me. "Just be patient. The time will come."

"Ok, ok, Mr. Andrews, I trust you!"

We looked on as the feed pellets disappeared with each white flash of a fish's side and the trailing surface swirl. A white farm truck passed slowly by, honked its horn, and a hand shot out of the window in an exaggerated, friendly wave.

"I guess you know everyone around here, huh?" I mused.

"That's how it is when you live your life in a small community. Everybody's a neighbor."

I thought of the expression for one to give the shirt off his back. Sitting by my side was a man who brought life to that saying. I knew that he would help anyone who came to him in need. He lived the saying without trying. I was proud to call Mr. Andrews my friend but even more proud for him to call me his friend.

After sitting and talking for a while longer, we

made our way back up the hill to the white house. Tidbit was sitting up on his chest looking around with a dazed expression. Mr. Andrews knelt down to pet him.

"You doin' alright, Tidbit? Now you don't have to worry about someone grabbing you by the tail!"

Inside the house I followed Mr. Andrews to the blue couch. I loved this couch. It was next to the treasure drawer, where Mr. Andrews kept his favorite knives. My mind was more childlike when I saw him reach to open the deep, wood drawer. Holding those amazing, one of a kind, handmade knives was a gift to me. Being able to run my thumb gently across the smooth blade, to touch the sharp tip delicately, to slide my finger across the various antler surface terrain, elicited emotions and provoked thought. I plopped down to Mr. Andrews' right side as he searched through the knife drawer. He took out a slab handle knife with a deeply polished yellow antler section on each side, one that I had not seen before. Fairly large at nine inches total length, it was one of the largest I had seen that he had made.

"Wow!" I exclaimed. "I didn't know you could make a slab handle knife out of whitetail antler."

"It took a big antler, Dr. Curtis, one with a lot of mass. And it had to be good and straight. See, I just split the antler down the center right there, and I still had plenty of room for the screws. I wanted it to look like those stag handle knives you see from Germany. It's a little bit bigger than any knife I like to use, but I just wanted to see if I could make it."

The shape of the handle and curve of the blade were ergonomically designed for left or right hands. This knife was a masterfully crafted breed of its own.

"Where are the imperfections in this knife?" I joked.

"Oh, if you look hard enough you will find them," he smiled sheepishly realizing the knife was nearly perfect.

As amazed as I was by this knife, I was even more amazed by the fact that this was a knife I had never seen before. The drawer seemed bottomless, like an endless treasure chest of one of a kind knives.

Shifting his legs to the right, he twisted his torso to look me in the eyes and said rather seriously, "You remember that day we started your dad's and father-in-law's knives? Well... I was going to tell you that most people don't stick with knife making. Everyone else I have tried to teach pretty much lost interest after one or two knives. It's hard. It takes time and patience. But you never know what you can do until you try. I thought then that you would stick with it, but I didn't want to be wrong. I decided to see if we really could finish both of those knives by Christmas. Sure enough, we did, Dr. Curtis! And I'm proud of that."

I sat stunned trying to process what I heard. Never had I considered not returning after my first knife was completed. Mr. Andrews was my friend, and I hoped he could feel that from me.

Feebly, I managed a brief response: "I just appreci-ate your willingness to teach me."

With a quick reply he spoke, "I appreciate your willingness to learn from me."

CHAPTER 6:

"Distance never tarnishes a friendship, Dr. Curtis."

I had made up my mind. Today would be the day I would tell him. Subconsciously, I guess the weather had a hand in the timing. This mid-February day bore down cold and dreary with a drizzling rain. After parking my truck, I sat staring out the rain splattered windshield at the white house before me. Opening the truck door quickly, I dashed the short distance to the screen porch. My arrival was heralded by the sharp crack of the slamming screen door. As I bent over to pull off my wet boots, the kitchen door opened with a creak, and Mr. Andrews warmly greeted me.

"Hey, Dr. Curtis, it's a cold one today, isn't it?"

"Yes sir, it sure is. We might be spending most of the day inside," I replied disappointedly.

"I think these old hands of mine can handle it," he grinned back. "Come on in and have some hot tea to warm up before we go out to the barn."

Automatically, I walked the few paces to my chair at the table, and Mrs. Nell came in the room to hug me.

Over a mug of hot flavored tea complemented with crackers and pepper jelly, Mr. Andrews asked, "You about finished with your elk knife?"

"Well, I've run into a bit of a problem. I got it out in the truck if you don't mind helping me with it."

Of course I knew he didn't mind. He anticipated it. Since starting my elk knife a month prior, I had returned numerous occasions to visit Mr. Andrews and to get help with the knife.

"When I set the blade in the handle, too much of the back of the blade was sticking out above the handle." I drew an imaginary pattern with my index finger on his table to better explain my error.

"Don't worry, Dr. Curtis. I know just what to do," he winked in reassurance.

I smiled back but was distracted by another thought. I tried to speak but found my tongue unable to make the words. My heart pounded in my ears and temple.

Thankfully, Mr. Andrews broke my verbal hiatus when he suggested, "Let's go have a look. Won't take long."

"Yes sir, that would be great." I swallowed hard and rose from the table.

Outside the cold, damp air cut through my clothes. The rain had turned to a heavy mist. Upon retrieving my elk knife from my truck, I hurried with Mr. Andrews to the work barn.

"Let me see that knife," Mr. Andrews motioned to me.

I handed it over for his inspection.

"Oh yes, I see exactly what we will do. In fact, I don't know if you could have done it better if you tried."

The perplexed look on my face gave away my lack of comprehension.

"Look right here," he said while covering part of the back of the blade with his calloused thumb. "I'm going to grind this down into a thumb groove to make it flush with the antler and bolster. You are going to love how this knife will handle when we are done."

The low hum of the grinding wheel started, and Mr. Andrews delicately touched the back of the blade to it for a few seconds and pulled back. He repeated this intermittent pattern until the thumb groove was cut into its proper position. Picking up a small handheld drimmel, he cut nine neat, evenly spaced notches in the thumb groove.

"These are for looks and to give your thumb traction while you are using the knife."

He held the knife slightly above his head to inspect, slowly turning it on its axis in order to examine all parts.

"You aren't too cold are you?" he asked caringly.

"No sir, I'm good if you are." Truth be told I was uncomfortably cold but couldn't admit it.

"Let's go ahead and touch this to the belt sander and then buff it out, and we will be finished with this knife," he said.

Stepping out of the work barn, we could hear a racket coming from the pecan trees above us. A fine mist fell from the dark, low clouds. In the damp trees were dozens upon dozens of robins chattering loudly to one another, apparently oblivious to the dismal weather conditions. I was certain the birds had not been there before. Mr. Andrews stood still and gazed upward, shielding his eyes with his left hand. As I studied the scene above, I realized that I could not find a single pecan leaf still on the tree. As strange as it may seem, I had, since the first visit, paid close attention to the pecan leaves above the house. Oddly enough, I had symbolically linked Mr. Andrews to this product of nature. Perhaps because on the first visit in October, the colored, withering leaves reminded me of Mr. Andrews, nearing the end of his life but still possessing enough zest to stand out like the autumn colors, still strong enough to weather more storms.

A small limb, dislodged by a fluttering robin, somersaulted to the ground and landed at the base of the tree with a muffled thud. There around the trunk of the tree, I viewed the unmistakable yellow of daffodils, "a host of golden daffodils" (to quote the 19th century poet William Wordsworth). The thin, dark green leaf blades sprouting from winter's ground mixed with the newly opened, fragrant, yellow buds of each flower proved a welcoming contrast to the gray February day. At once I saw myself in these early harbingers of spring. Not even three years into my professional career and just over two years of marriage, I was beginning to navigate the paths of life. I was young and hardy, able to withstand the cold and freeze that winter might throw at me like the blooming daffodil.

My thoughts turned to the present, and I resumed my walk, trailing Mr. Andrews to the kitchen house. A meow was heard, though faint, and I searched the grounds for Tidbit. Under the kitchen house near the crooked wooden steps, Tidbit ventured out enough to be seen. I squatted to rub his ears, but he was reluctant to expose his whole body to the wet air. Tidbit watched as we entered the little building, too fearful to ever investigate inside because of the tool's din. Mr. Andrews sat down in the metal chair, turned on the one inch belt sander, and worked the newly formed thumb groove of the blade back and forth with short strokes. His hands, so tough and calloused, performed the intricate task of maneuvering the belt evenly into the curved groove. I became absorbed in the motions of his hands. His hands looked as tanned as they would have been on a summer's day, but this color was cumulative. These hands were of a working man's, having survived the ravages of life's storms. The cold could not penetrate this stubborn skin to constrict the blood vessels enough to change the hands' appearance. My hands, however, were shockingly pale with an almost blue hue around the fingertips. They were icy to the touch and throbbed with the sting of the cold. If Mr. Andrews' hands were chilled, then he never gave away a hint of it.

During a pause, he studied the winter's landscape out the open door. The yard seemed devoid of shadows, so thick were the low, gray clouds obscuring the sun's light.

Removing his camouflage cap from his bald head with a long sigh, he reasoned, "This weather can sure put a damper on fishing."

I realized that he was looking at the pond in view through the open doorway.

"That's ok though. Spring will be here before we know it. It will be time to fish in Pataula Creek."

"Where's that?" I asked.

"Over at Lake Eufaula. I got a honeyhole there that I'm not sure anyone else knows about. I can catch a whole heap of bass there. There's a sandy spot that drops off real deep. The bass usually hit a small, white spinnerbait."

"I would like to see that spot," unintentionally inviting myself.

"You'll just have to go with me sometime," he offered.

I smiled at the idea and gave an affirmative head nod in agreement.

"Ok, Dr. Curtis, all you have to do is buff this thing out and your job is done. It's going to be a fine knife. What do you say we go inside and warm up?"

I attempted to downplay my eagerness for warmth.

Inside the toasty, dimly lit house, we made our way to the couch. Mrs. Nell was sitting in her chair with a sleepy look on her face. My heart began to beat faster, and my breathing grew shallow. It was time to reveal my plans to Mr. Andrews. Before I could confess, Mr. Andrews opened the magic side table drawer to withdraw a shiny, deep brown knife sheath. Dark brown streaks coursed through the pale leather backdrop. There was an antique style to its appearance.

He presented the sheath to me and said, "What do you think?"

Failing to comprehend the gesture, I replied, "It's nice, Mr. Andrews. Where's the knife for it?"

He laughed and said, "See if your elk knife fits."

Surprised, I hopped up to go grab my knife I had set on the dining table. I slid the knife in and snapped the latch shut. The snap caught effortlessly, and I blurted out, "It's perfect! It fits perfectly. When did you... how did you... how did you know it would fit? I mean, last time I was here I hadn't even set the blade yet!"

A wink of his eye brought forth the secret of his accomplishment.

"All I did was hold the pieces in place last time you were here and molded and measured the leather from there. I did have to assume a little, but I figured I knew how you would do it. I did it, of course, while you weren't watching."

"This is incredible, Mr. Andrews. I really appreciate

your making this sheath for me. You will have to show me how you get those streaks in the leather like that," I said tracing a line on the leather with my finger.

"It's not hard. Next time we make one, I will show you my little trick."

I stared at the opposite wall with a returning feeling of dread. I needed to tell him now, but how quickly my tongue became dry and refused to articulate the message. I willed my lips to move, and at last the words spilled out in the most ungraceful flow.

"Mr. Andrews... I'm... um...well... I'm moving away."

There was a swift release of my tension as I let the words go. Mr. Andrews stared back at me for a moment, and I think he could see the concern on my face. I had only known this man four months, and we had created a friendship unlike any I had ever had or would have. Now I would be relocating my life. No longer could I drive over on a Wednesday afternoon to visit, nor expect to be there at least once weekly as had become my custom.

With an understanding, reassuring voice, he calmly said, "Distance never tarnishes a friendship, Dr. Curtis. So, just where are you moving to?"

"Over to a little town east of Tifton... Alapaha."

"Oh, I know where Alapaha is. It's only about two and a half hours from here," he said optimistically.

"It's just that I really look forward to coming over here." I said pitifully. "And I know I won't be able to come as often as I do now."

"I have a feeling you will still come to visit this old man," he laughed trying to lighten the mood. "When's the move date?"

"Not sure yet but sometime in May."

"That's great, Dr. Curtis. You will still be here when the fish really get to biting." Both of us laughed at that.

Changing the subject, I pointed to the drawer and said, "You got any more knives to show me in there?"

He withdrew my favorite highly polished mule deer knife and placed it in my hand, knowing that I loved that knife. As I held the smooth yellow grip with the dark longitudinal lines, Mr. Andrews removed several more knives, and we made small talk. Occasionally, Mrs. Nell would add to the conversation. I realized sweet Mrs. Nell had not said a word about my moving away.

Finally, I stood to leave and Mrs. Nell said, "You know you are always welcome here. We have a spare bedroom with your own bathroom too."

I thanked her graciously before exiting the room. Mr. Andrews followed me outside like he had done all the times before. Tidbit sat on his rump at the base of the steps and meowed at me. I pet his head, and the lump in my throat grew. I was fighting back tears. This was a place I loved, almost like a step back in time to my childhood. There was a soothing, peaceful sense when I came here. I tried to inhale slowly, but the frigid air stung my nostrils. In the fading gray light, I could barely make out the tree branches above. No more chattering robins. Without turning around, I walked briskly to my truck. I knew Mr. Andrews was behind me.

Opening the door of my truck, I faced Mr. Andrews and extended my hand to shake his goodbye.

"I really appreciate the sheath you made me." I choked out hoarsely.

His handshake was firm and warm and prolonged. He rocked my hand slowly back and forth looking me in the eyes.

With a slight smile he said, "Come back when you can, Dr. Curtis."

I bit my lip, nodded my head, and hopped into my truck. Then the tears fell.

CHAPTER 7:

"Always remember, this is some special steel right here."

My fishing pole leaned against the wall next to my tackle box in the laundry room. Lifting both, I enthusiastically dashed out of our small rental house into the welcoming spring air. A sweet fragrance perfused the warm late April day, like a thousand different flowers bottled together to produce one memory stimulating aroma. And oh what music! No season of the year did the birds sing more garrulously. The mockingbird flaunted its ability to diversify song above the rest, but all chimed in to produce a synchronized sound of nature. Getting in my truck, I drove westward into a magnificent panorama of fresh, vibrant colors. The morning sun was already well above the tree tops behind me and cast a slanting orange glow on the terrain before me. The deep blue sky directly overhead faded into a softer, lighter blue as it reached toward the western horizon and seemed to gently restrain the far-away, wispy, pink-white clouds from approaching any farther. Rounding the sharp curve in front of the Andrews' home, I slowed to turn into the first entrance by the pond. I had become accustomed to entering this first driveway because often times Mr. Andrews was sitting by his pond. Today was no different.

"Hey, Mr. Andrews!" I yelled through the open truck window while still rolling. "I brought my fishing stuff today."

"Good! I can smell some bream beds. They ought to be biting today."

Parking my truck near the pond, I threw open the door, hopped out, and immediately picked up my fishing rod and tackle box out of the truck bed.

"What you got tied on?" he asked.

"Just an old tried and true plastic worm. I wanted to try to catch some bass this time."

"Go around there to that corner by the dam," he pointed with an outstretched arm. "See that oak limb hanging over? There's always a bass under it."

Sure enough, first cast I felt two thumps on my line. I slowly reeled down on the slack in the line, and then with a rapid jerk of the rod, I set the hook securely into the bass's mouth. The frisky fish leaped acrobatically out of the water like a tarpon as I fought him to the grassy bank.

"Nice fish!" Mr. Andrews shouted from down the way. "Keep him to clean if you want to."

"It's alright, Mr. Andrews, I'm going to catch and release today."

Mr. Andrews reached to the ground and picked up his fishing pole equipped with a small beetle spin lure with a black and yellow plastic grub on the hook. I made another cast near the overhanging limb and heard loud splashing to my left. Mr. Andrews had hooked into a large bream that was thrashing on the water's surface. The wiggly fish was yanked from the water at the bank and into Mr. Andrews' awaiting hand.

"Dr. Curtis, I ever tell you about trying to take my mother-in-law fishing?"

"No sir," I replied, not catching on that he was setting up a joke.

"I always told her that I believed in drowning my sorrows." He paused several seconds. "But she never would go fishing with me!!" He cackled in laughter while he unhooked the bream and tossed the fish back into the water.

I became tickled myself, more so at Mr. Andrews' reaction to his own joke. Humorously, I responded, "I don't know why on earth she wouldn't want to fish with you then!"

Several more bass fell victim to my lure along the dam, and then I fished my way back toward Mr. Andrews. He had taken a seat in one of the two metal folding chairs. Tidbit had made his way to the base of the chair and watched the pond lazily. I sat down in the empty chair and set my rod down. The sun was shining hotly, but a low humidity helped to counteract the heat. A soft breeze blew just strong enough to produce a slight washboard appearance on the pond. Cows mooed hollowly in the distance. Nearby in the pines a bobwhite quail whistled its sharp tune in hopes of finding a companion. The pecan trees were laden with bright green new growth sprouting forth from their branches. We sat, Mr. Andrews and I, for some time without words, taking in the beauty and calm around us.

After resuming conversation for a while, Mr. Andrews peered over his shoulder at Tidbit scratching in the recently planted garden plot.

"Come on, Dr. Curtis. Let me show you my garden." Pushing himself slowly off the chair, he walked to the rectangular red dirt spot and said, "These two rows are my corn--sweet corn. Right there's my squash. Here's okra... eggplant. Tomato plants over there."

The crops were mere tiny green projections from the earth in neat rows, undistinguishable with an untrained eye. I sensed the joy that Mr. Andrews received from his green thumb, and for each plant he explained the growing requirements and particulars. My mind was desperately trying to trap the information it was being fed, but I could not will it all to stick.

"What do you say we go eat us a sandwich?" He suggested, nodding his head toward the house.

Finishing our lunch, Mr. Andrews took me into the spare bedroom and opened the top dresser drawer revealing several small clear tackle boxes. Inside each was a collection of fishing jigs of assorted colors and sizes.

Snapping open two plastic locking tabs, he opened one of the lids.

"You ever seen a jig like this?" he asked me while picking up a black, brown, gray, and white fishing jig with his thumb and forefinger.

"Looks like fur of some kind," I concluded.

"That's right. Squirrel tail. It makes a mighty fine fishing lure. Easy to make too. Here, I'll show you."

Taking a squirrel tail from a plastic bag, he trimmed off a tuft of fur about two inches long and began wrapping it around a bare jig head with a strand of waxed synthetic sinew. He then put a dab of epoxy on the wrapped sinew and placed it on a piece of wax paper to dry.

"And that's all there is to it. One of the best bream lures you could ask for. Take these. I want you to have plenty."

At that, Mr. Andrews put five in a bag and handed them to me. "So you brought a knife you are working on?"

"Yes sir, got it out in the truck. I'm making it for my best friend. I got an antler off a buck he shot when he was a kid, so I think he will really like it."

We walked out of the house through the slamming screen door, and down to the bright, green pond where my truck still sat. Opening my truck's center console, I brought out the partially completed knife with a smooth, white, almost ivory sheen antler handle.

Mr. Andrews turned the knife slowly over to view

all sides and said while not looking away, "You don't have a chance in this life to have too many best friends, you know? You say you are making this for Cole?" I knew I had not said specifically that I was referring to Cole, but I had known Mr. Andrews long enough now that he knew who my best friend was. Mr. Andrews liked Cole and his family very much and was especially acquainted with Cole's granddad, Billy, who farmed thousands of acres in the county. Andrews Drilling Company had put in many irrigation wells for Mr. Billy. Mr. Andrews would laugh and say that he was never worried when Billy owed him money because it was just as good as money in the bank.

"Yes sir." I replied to his question.

"That's a good family, Dr. Curtis. Good people. They will do anything for you."

Up the hill we went to the work barn, past the multicolored pepper plants in their oversized black pots. Past the tall pecan trees with their daffodils guarding the trunks, the daffodils now nothing more than thick bladed grass without evidence of bloom. The flowers had long since withered and shrunk back into the hardy bulbs. Inside the barn Mr. Andrews guided me through some methods to enhance the knife's details.

"Well, Dr. Curtis, how 'bout some pepper jelly?"

Of course, it was our routine.

With our bellies greedily satisfied with crackers, pepper jelly, and sweet tea, we found ourselves relaxing on the old, comfortable, blue couch. Since walking into the room, I had noticed on the side table a small rectangular piece of steel that was covered completely in rust. A brief lull in our talking prompted Mr. Andrews to pick up the piece of steel with his sun-blotched, wrinkled fingers.

"I think I showed this to you already, but it's the same piece of steel that I made my two mule deer knives out of. Only enough left for one more small knife." He paused and stared at the unimpressive stick of rust. "You know, Dr. Curtis, this is the best little piece of cutting steel I've ever had. I'm sure it's the oldest too. I had enough originally to make three nice sized knives. Wanted them to be unlike any I had made before. That's why I used mule deer antler... the only time I have used mule deer antler. As you know, I made one to use for cleaning catfish, and boy have I used that knife... still gotta find that ole knife to show you one of these days. I will keep on looking. And the other one, well, it's right here in this drawer beside me. Never been used. I just look at it from time to time. I never could decide what type of knife to make for the third. Definitely wanted it to be special and unique. Oh, I've had some ideas but never could bring myself to commit. Now I'm 81. Life goes like that. It will pass you by before you know it."

He took a deep breath and readjusted his glasses with his left hand. Shifting slightly on the soft cushion, he looked me in the eyes. "Dr. Curtis, I want you to make a good little knife out of this. Always remember, this is some special steel right here."

"Is it the Carnegie steel?" I blurted out.

He smiled at me, "Might be..."

"But I feel bad taking this from you..."

He interrupted, "I'm giving it to you. I want you to have it."

I stammered, "It's just that, I'm scared I'm going to mess it up and then that's it. There is none left."

"You won't mess it up," he laughed caringly. "No knife is perfect. And anyway, it's better to leave imperfections, remember?" He winked back at me.

"What kind of knife should I make?" I asked in an almost desperate tone.

"I'm going to leave that up to you to decide, Dr. Curtis."

As we continued to talk on the couch, I distractedly thought of the rusted steel in my hand. The afternoon was getting late, and I knew I had to get back home. I also knew this would be my last visit before moving away. However, there was a cheerful, peaceful atmosphere around us. I had prepared myself for a sorrowful departure, but to my surprise, the feeling never came. Mr. Andrews, like always, walked me to my truck still parked down the hill by the calm pond. The sun's angled rays beamed off the pond's surface to irradiate the brilliant green oak branches before us. So beautiful. So calming. No sorrow. I looked Mr. Andrews in the eyes and shook his hand tightly.

"Dr. Curtis, come back when you can."

This time no tears fell.

CHAPTER 8:

"I'm not sure why people like my knives so much."

To quote the country singer, Tracy Byrd, the day was "hot enough to make the devil sigh." On this July 14th day, the temperature at 9 AM was in the low 80s with a humidity of upper 90%. I struck out due west like so many times before to go see the knife maker, but instead of the relatively quick twenty minute, scenic drive as before, I was journeying two and a half hours. The sun was high above and burned mercilessly down on me as I arrived at my destination. The old, towering pecan trees could not disguise the withering heat stress its leaves had endured. There was nearly an autumn appearance to the desiccated, yellow-tinted foliage. Tidbit was lazily lounging in the shade of a foundation shrub. Inside the house the air was cool and refreshing as the Andrews happily greeted me in the kitchen. I was directed to my chair at the dinner table where a sandwich, pear salad, and iced tea awaited me. In spite of numerous phone conversations over the last two months, we had much to discuss since my move.

"So you are working in Tifton now?"

"Yes sir, I enjoy it so far there. We have five vets besides me, so the workload is spread out pretty good.

And we have rotating days off during the week, which gives me time to work on my knives." I laughed: "People are learning that I make knives, so I have a pretty healthy waiting list of requests. Right now I'm making one for an auction to benefit a guy fighting cancer; he lives near Albany."

Mr. Andrews smiled wide, and his eyes lit up at my mentioning an auction.

"But I don't think it's going to go for $3500 like yours!"

We both laughed and then he said, "No, gotta work your way up to that kind of price, but I bet this first one you do will surprise you. Probably be $250-300 or so I imagine."

A look of skepticism crept over my face: "I will be lucky if it's in the triple digits!"

"We will see, Dr. Curtis, we will see." (And he was correct in his assumption. My knife auctioned for $250.)

After eating, Mr. Andrews suggested we go to one of his hang out spots to evade the oppressive summer heat. Hopping into his white Chevy S-10 pickup truck, we took a winding, hilly route to Worthy Auto Parts in the nearby town of Edison. The parts store was immediately adjacent to a mechanic shop, and it sure looked like "the place to be," judging from the number of cars and trucks parked out front. As I followed Mr. Andrews through the glass door, a group of older men at the checkout counter hollered rambunctiously at Mr. Andrews. He turned to me grinning.

"This is a pretty rowdy crowd, Dr. Curtis. I guess I call them friends," he laughed and spoke loud enough for all in the room to hear.

Laughter erupted from the group of men. I was introduced as "Dr. Curtis," and I self-consciously interjected, "I'm Andrew." We talked for a few minutes before I thought to inquire about Mark Davis.

"He's in the garage next door," said the owner, Terry Worthy, a tall, older man with glasses and a stern face.

"I'm going to go tell him hey," I reported while making my way to a side door.

My friendship with Mr. Andrews likely would have never come about were it not for this man. Mark Davis was a master mechanic by trade but also a hunt guide at a quail preserve in his spare time. Occasionally, Mark would bring dogs to the vet clinic in Albany where I had previously worked. As personable as he was, we became well acquainted, and I even had the privilege of quail hunting with him. One day in September 2012, one month prior to meeting Mr. Andrews, Mark walked into the vet clinic toting a very large whitetail shed antler he had found on Rio Piedra Quail Preserve. I told him about my passion for shed hunting and about the antler collection I possessed. Coincidentally, I confided to Mark that I had a desire to learn to make an antler handle knife, and he quickly informed me of Mr. Andrews and gave me his phone number.

"Doc, is that you?" Mark said in his Southern twang, coming over to shake my hand.

"Yes sir! Mr. Andrews brought me here for a little while because we decided it was too hot to do much outside right now."

"You right about that! How you been? I heard you moved to Tifton."

"Yeah, I actually moved to Alapaha, east of Tifton, but I do work in Tifton. I already miss seeing you quail guys."

Mr. Andrews poked his head through the door and yelled, "Mark, what you doin' talkin' and not workin'?!"

He couldn't suppress the smile as Mark playfully retorted, "Aw, c'mon, Mr.Edwin, you know I never rest."

We talked and joked for a few minutes before Mark said, "Hold on, I'll be right back." He returned with a large antler and handed it to me. "It's the match to the one I gave you last year."

He had given me the big antler on the day he had told me of Mr. Andrews, and now I had the magnificent pair from a huge South Georgia whitetail. Expressing my gratitude, we left Mark to continue his work, walked back through the side door, and sat with the guys in the parts store, trying to whittle away time from the mid afternoon's scorching temperatures.

Navigating the curvy road back to his home, Mr. Andrews exclaimed, "It's about time for some pepper jelly and iced tea, isn't it?"

"Yes sir, I could go for that," I smacked my dry lips.

The day was still sticky and hot, but the shadows were beginning to stretch across the yard when we turned into his driveway. The cold tea with crackers and pepper jelly was satisfyingly thirst quenching and delivered a welcoming reprieve from the day's heat.

Finishing off the last swallow of tea with a fulfilled sigh, Mr. Andrews said, "Let's go get your knife for the auction and see if we can touch it up a bit."

Making our way across the yard to the barn, sweat instantaneously trickled down my back. The air in the barn was warm and stale even with the doors flung open. Ignoring the heat, Mr. Andrews skillfully modified my blade's shape in a subtle approach. I knew he did not want to alter my design too much because it was my project, and he respected that. I, however, was never offended by any suggestion of change he might have made. He was the master at this game.

"Who's this knife for, Dr. Curtis?"

"Mark Cody. Works at Tarva. He's got testicular cancer, and it has spread. I'm not sure of his chances."

"Cancer is a bad thing. You never know what tomorrow will bring. It's a blessing every day to wake up healthy." He polished on the antler handle for a few minutes and admiringly remarked, "This is a fine knife you made, Dr. Curtis. It's going to surprise you in the auction." Giving the knife to me he said, "Let's go feed my catfish."

Down by the pond the weeds grew wild and unruly so much so that we had to trample them underfoot to sidle up to the bank. As the feed pellets hit the water, the calm surface erupted into a frenzy of splashing.

"I sure do love catfish. It's got to be my favorite fish to eat. One of these days I'm going to make you my Almost Famous Catfish Stew." Then a jocular grin slowly worked its way over his face, "But only on a special occasion..."

"I know, I know," I jokingly replied, rolling my eyes. "I guess I will just keep on waiting until that special day comes."

"All in good time, Dr. Curtis."

The shade from the pine trees provided us a cooler spot to stand, but the absence of wind permitted the stifling heat to continue to envelop us. Mr. Andrews removed his cap to wipe the sweat off his forehead with his sleeve. Instinctively, I mirrored his motions.

"Let's go in out of this heat," he suggested. "Got something I want to show you."

Nearly every visit he had "something to show me," and whatever it was never ceased to amaze me. Following merrily along, I tried to figure out what "something" would be this time.

Collapsing on the cool couch with a fatigued grunt, Mr. Andrews slid open the magic side drawer. I found myself leaning towards him trying to peek inside. Delicately he lifted a dirty white rag out of the drawer, unraveled it, and displayed a knife. The antler handle was as colorful as I had ever seen. He had sanded and polished it in such a way that the colors seemed to melt into each other. The dark, heavy browns faded into orange, then yellow, and then finally into an exhilaratingly bright white. His characteristic red, white, and black spacers were neatly fitted between the handle and the glistening nickel silver bolster. A simple blade with a straight spine was so perfectly polished that I could not find a scratch mark. In the middle across one side of the blade was professionally inscribed GAGwP-2013 (Georgia Associaton of Groundwater Professionals), and parallel to the bolster were the letters EHA—his initials.

At that moment the realization hit me. Mr. Andrews and I both had been working on a knife to auction off for a cause, but oh what a difference in quality! Mine was crude and elementary; his was masterful and professional. Here was a man nearly 82 years old producing handmade knives of utmost quality far beyond what machines could do. I stared at his hands, then at mine, then back at his. Those fingers, stiff, wrinkled, calloused, and sun-blotched, were such a stark contrast to my pale, smooth, and nimble fingers. His fingers were powerfully driven by years of experience, a lifetime of fifty-four years more than mine. It is the motor that makes the car run. In that moment I was humbly aware of my inexperience, not just in knife making but also in life itself.

"Mr. Andrews, how do you do it?! This knife is as near to perfect as you can get it."

He laughed, "There are plenty of imperfections. Just look." I shook my head in disbelief: "I don't see any. I wonder how much this knife will auction for?"

"I'm not sure why people like my knives so much. They are nothing special. But people love to bid on them." He paused and stared at his creation.

I knew why people liked these knives so much, or at least one of the reasons why. Everyone who owned one of Mr. Andrews' knives and knew the kind of person he was felt a connection through the knife to Mr. Andrews himself. His morals. His ethics. His generosity. His humility. His faith. His love. All of this went into his knives. He transformed a simple, inanimate tool into a treasure trove of emotional stimuli. Sure, I loved the knives for what they were, but I loved their creator immensely more.

"Well, Mr. Andrews, I got a little bit of a drive to make, so I better hit the road."

He walked me out of the house, through the slamming screen door, down the steps, and to my truck. Asking to see my auction knife once more, he carefully inspected the contours by running his fingers along its edges.

"Yes sir," he remarked convincingly. "Someone is going to be proud to get this knife." Just before I climbed into the truck, he pointed to my right hip and said, "That knife treating you right?"

I had worn on my belt the first antler knife he had made me.

"Of course! I love it. I didn't know if you had seen it on me or not."

He chuckled, "I noticed it as soon as I saw you today. I'm glad you like it." He shook my hand firmly like he always would. "Come back when you can, Dr. Curtis."

CHAPTER 9:

"Thanks for being a good friend."

E very few weeks or so I would make the two and a half hour drive west to go visit my old friend. We stayed in consistent phone contact, but on the first of October, I received a letter from Mr. Andrews. It would be the first of two and the only one of any length. Dated September 29, 2013, the handwritten note read:

Dr. Curtis,

I haven't written a letter in years. I guess my grammar is about like Frank and Earnest. Frank: "Can you make a sentence using the word 'fascinate'?" Earnest: "My jacket has nine buttons, but I can only fasten eight." Frank: "Can you make a sentence using the word 'acquire'?" Earnest: "The girl loved to sing, so she joined a choir." Frank: "Earnest, I don't know about your grammar." Earnest: "Grandma is fine, but I have an aunt that is really sick."

We had a birthday for Vickie (Harold's wife) Saturday night. Amy and Grant (Amy's husband) were there. Amy announced the baby's name—Andrew. Her time is down to about three weeks.

Dr. Curtis, Nell and I really enjoyed your visit last Thurs. Come back when you can stay and cook fish. We had some Fri. night. They were mighty good. I am well pleased that I could share my little bit of knife ability with you. I think it is a good hobby because it leaves you something to show for your time. Most people won't try knifemaking because when they see the end result, they automatically assume there is no way they could do it. You don't know what you can do until you try.

Come when you can. May the good Lord keep and bless you.

Your friend,
Edwin H. Andrews (signature)

This letter encompassed who Mr. Andrews is- a man of humor, love, family pride, generosity, humbleness, motivation, and faith, with a conscious understanding and appreciation of friendship. When I gazed upon his cursive signature, I could envision more than simply a name written in pen on paper. I saw the unblemished name, a name which Amy and Grant had chosen to honor by naming their first born Andrew. (Coincidentally we share the same name.) That was the man I could model my life after. He had taught me an enormous amount already, but I could not fathom just how much more he would teach me.

Each time I went to see Mr. Andrews I was working on a different knife, and occasionally he would be making another of his own. Through repetition I became more efficient in my techniques, but no matter how confident I felt in my work, I realized Mr. Andrews always had a trick that I had yet to learn.

However, the visits yielded more than knife sessions. I was gradually learning parallel lessons in life. Mr. Andrews was shaping my character like he would transform a piece of rusty metal into a beautifully polished knife blade.

In September 2014, Mr. Andrews mailed me a package with ten various sized squirrel tail jigs he had made. A handwritten note was attached.

> *Dr. Curtis,*
> *I know these jigs are a little crude, but they <u>will catch</u> fish. My hands are not as nimble as they used to be. I will be 83 Oct. 13.*
> *Thanks for being a good friend,*
> *Edwin H. Andrews (signature)*

Two points struck me from this note. First, the fact that he felt the jigs were "crude." I thought the jigs were beautiful, simple yes, but beautiful. And yes, I knew first hand that these lures would catch fish well. Like the jigs, he thought his knives "crude," and perhaps they were simple in design but so magnificent and completely functional. Mr. Andrews was much like the knives he made, seemingly plain at first glance but quality to the core. The second point which truly humbled me was his thanking ME for being a good friend. Could he not see how high I regarded him? He gave, and I received. In character, he seemed to tower over me like the enormous pecan trees over his home. So short in physical stature but so enormously impacting in my life. The span of 54 years was no deterrent to our deep friendship. In fact, it was likely the spark.

CHAPTER 10:

"I knew I was going to give it to you one day."

The night air was cold and still. Even from within my small work shed, my exhaled breath could be seen. Exchanging the coarse sanding belt for a fine grit, I resumed my work, with determination to finish this knife by the morning.

At dawn I climbed into my chilly truck cab, and with the sun at my back, drove down the highway. It was a freezing start to this November 22nd day in 2014, five days before Thanksgiving. By the time my truck slowed around the familiar curve with the caddy cornered white house, the sun was high in the dark blue sky, and the temperature had risen to a comfortable level. Even though Mr. Andrews was not by the pond, I turned in the first driveway entrance to get a better look at the spectacular blue water colored by the brilliant fall sky above. I slowly eased the truck up the hill to park on the backside of the house, which was my custom. I felt the cool, circulating air on my face and in my nostril as I opened the truck door. I peered upward as I heard a faint rustle of leaves. The mighty pecan trees still harbored pockets of brown, wilted leaves, but the majority had joined on the ground to produce a crackling carpet on which to tread. Across the road the cows were standing silently in the sunlight acknowledging my arrival. Several timid cats scurried under the bushes while I noisily crunched my way to the screen door. Instinctively, my eyes looked for Tidbit, but I knew. Tidbit would not greet me today.

It would be the first visit that Tidbit would not be there. He was my official greeter. He was our tag-along friend. He was our fishing companion. He was a part of our visits. And now he was gone. Three weeks earlier, Mr. Andrews had called to tell me sadly that Tidbit had passed away. A stray dog had wandered into the yard and attacked him. I already felt his absence.

No sooner than I opened the screen door, the creaky kitchen door sprang open to reveal Mr. Andrews' inviting grin.

"Glad you could make it out today, Dr. Curtis. Come on inside."

He shook my hand and patted my left shoulder gently. I followed him to the den, which was cozily warmed by an electric heater.

Mrs. Nell was situated in her chair with a white blanket in her lap.

"I'm really glad you came, Andrew. Edwin has been looking forward to this all week," she said barely above a whisper.

She looked frail and tired. The sunlight poured

through the curtained windows behind her.

I sat down to Mr. Andrews' right on the couch and said, "I hate that about Tidbit. I'm really going to miss him."

Mr. Andrews looked toward the window with a sad smile. "He was a bad joker..."

The hurt look on his face prompted me to change the subject. "I sure have enjoyed those squirrel tail jigs you made me. I caught some nice bass in my pond on one. Those things hold up really well."

"I'm glad you like them," he replied happily. "I have certainly loved fishing with them through the years. Do you need any more? I got plenty in there," he said pointing to the spare bedroom where he stored some of his fishing tackle.

"No thanks. As durable as those jigs are, I ought to be good for a long time."

"What do you say we try them out in the pond after lunch?" he asked.

Our lunch consisted of tasty, leftover vegetable soup, rolls, and iced tea. Next, I found myself following Mr. Andrews down the hill toward the bright pond with fishing pole in hand and a newly tied squirrel tail jig on the end of my line. The doves were calling their peaceful, wooing song from high in the pines. I could make out a few of their tell-tale silhouettes dark against the radiant blue sky. The temperature was a pleasant 60 degrees in the sun. The cooling breeze was just strong enough to feel as a breath on my face but not enough to disturb the pond's calm surface. I could see a nice-sized catfish cruising lazily beneath the water's glare.

Mr. Andrews must have seen it too because he remarked, "Got plenty of good eatin' catfish in here that will be just right for some Almost Famous Catfish Stew. Boy, I sure do love that recipe."

"But it's got to be a special occasion only," I joked back.

We both laughed, and I cast my jig far out in the middle of the pond. As I slowly reeled my lure in, a heavy thump signaled a fish strike, so I jerked the rod automatically. The jig launched out of the water, and I had to duck my head to avoid an impact.

"Be patient, Dr. Curtis. Just let those bream take it a second before you set the hook. And try not to snatch it. Easy does it."

"Yes sir, I guess I got too excited," I said in an embarrassed tone.

Repeating my cast, I began a slow retrieve and felt the same firm thump on my line. I snatched... too soon! The jig sped towards my body once more, so I dodged the tiny projectile.

"Dang it," I groaned.

"It's ok, you got it. Just keep your rod low. When

the fish bites, stop reeling, then gently pull the rod to the side to set the hook, keeping the rod tip low."

"Third time's a charm," I thought. My jig made a long sweeping arc to land with a soft splash. I felt the tug almost instantly, stopped reeling, gave the fish some line slack, then casually pulled my rod tip, feeling the tension of my prize at the other end. Then the fight of the frisky fish began.

"There you go, Dr. Curtis! You got the hang of it now," Mr. Andrews yelled excitedly.

I thought I knew all the tricks to freshwater fishing. Since I was three years old, I had enjoyed fishing and thought myself very competent with a rod and reel in my hands, but Mr. Andrews proved that I could still learn a thing or two on the water.

The determined bluegill bream battled me to the weedy bank but submitted upon my plucking him from the water. No picture could replicate this fish's colors. Sunlight and a living, breathing moment were required to appreciate the indescribable colors of this wonderful fish. As I held the specimen, I realized that this was a "living in the moment" situation. Before unhooking the beautiful pan fish, I glanced to my left at a grinning Mr. Andrews. So happy. We both were. Thanksgiving wafted in the air, and in that moment, we were truly thankful for so much at once. Two friends brought together-- the present negated the past or the future, carving a memory for both of us to share.

I gently tossed the fish back into the pond, and we resumed our fishing.

Only after many more dark bluegills had been caught, Mr. Andrews asked with a raise of his eyebrows, "It's about time for some pepper jelly. What do you think?"

Up the hill, side by side we walked, up the concrete steps, through the screen door, and into the kitchen. I walked to the dining table while Mr. Andrews collected the snack supplies. Over our crackers, cream cheese, pepper jelly, and hot tea, Mr. Andrews filled me in on his family: Harold, Amy, Mark, and his precious one year old great grandson, Andrew. At some point I had realized that at these times over crackers and pepper jelly, Mr. Andrews talked happily about his family. No time did I visit that we did not sit at that dining table with pepper jelly.

Mr. Andrews slid his chair away from the table and said, "Come on, I want to show you the knife I'm working on. It's a wooden slab handle."

Out to the work barn we went.

Picking up a nearly completed wood handled knife, Mr. Andrews handed it to me for inspection.

"What kind of wood is this, Mr. Andrews?"

"Ironwood. It's like it sounds--tough. I'm making this for Harold and Vickie to use in the kitchen."

The dark brown wood contoured to my palm in a soothing way. In order to replicate this knife, I took a picture like I had done with most of his knives.

"You like that, huh? I got some more ironwood right over there in the corner," he said pointing to a dark corner of the barn next to the rusty saw blades. I bent over to retrieve a piece of the wood. "Take all of it, Dr. Curtis. I can get more if I need it."

"Oh, I don't want to take all you have…"

"Take it. I want you to have it."

I did not argue anymore. We chatted for a while, gazing across the road to the sunlit pasture where the cows were on their feet grazing. Without word of where we were going, Mr. Andrews led me back to the house and inside to the couch.

We plopped down beside each other, and he asked me expectantly: "You bring that knife you are working on?"

"Yes sir, I sure did!" Unable to suppress my excitement, my fingers fumbled in my coat pocket for the leather sheath. I was giddy as I handed the knife and sheath to Mr. Andrews.

He extracted the small knife from its case and rolled the knife slowly in his hands.

"Dr. Curtis, I knew you could do it. You made the knife that I never made… the third and final…"

He beamed proudly at me through his thick glasses. I was a bit stunned. I had been careful not to mention that I was working on a knife using the old "Carnegie steel." I figured I would surprise him with the news after he had a chance to peruse the knife.

I stammered, "I... I... how did you know that was the steel I used?"

A sly expression formed on his face. "I guess you could say I picked up on some clues. You really did a fine job, Dr. Curtis."

At that he leaned to his left, opened the wooden table drawer and brought out the beautiful, smooth, yellow-streaked mule deer knife-- the one I loved so much, the one that had the same old "Carnegie steel" as the knife I had recently made. There was one significant difference this time in the mule deer knife. Immediately, I noticed the brass bolster and end cap were brightly polished and unmistakably shiny. Mr. Andrews held both knives side by side and stared for several minutes--just stared. No words. His expression serious. Then a smile softened his wrinkled face.

"I want you to have my mule deer knife. It goes with this knife you just made."

"Mr. Andrews, I can't take that knife." I said regrettably, knowing that knife was my favorite of his. "Someone in your family might want it."

"No sir," he shook his head definitively. "I've made my family a whole heap of knives through the years. This knife is special to you. Well, it's special to both of us. I'm not sure anybody can understand and feel this knife like you. The first day you came to visit me, the first time I watched you hold this knife, I knew I was going to give it to you one day. You were drawn to it before I even had a chance to tell you how special it actually was."

He placed the knife in my hand. The smooth yellow handle with dark streaks. The shiny brass end plate and bolster. The straight-spine blade with a subtle upturned tip. The knife that I had longed to have but never dared to ask for. It was now mine but never would it not be his. The knife was a piece of him... and now a piece of me.

CHAPTER 11:

"So what do you think, Dr. Curtis?
Is it as good as you thought it would be?"

"You ready to try my Almost Famous Catfish
Stew?"

"I thought you would never ask!" I laughed while standing in the yard by the steps to the white house.

The day was partly cloudy, warm but pleasant. A fairly stiff breeze blew from the west. The occasion was certainly a special one. Today was October 13, 2015, Mr. Andrews' 84th birthday, the first birthday we had spent together since my first visit.

Talking to Mr. Andrews, I discovered that he had our entire day planned.

"We need to run into town and pick up some groceries. Hop in. I'll drive."

Obediently, I opened the door to Mr. Andrews' white S-10 pick-up truck, which reminded me of my grandfather's truck from twenty years ago. We set out north on a scenic country road to Cuthbert, and after a few minutes of driving, we passed by the most gorgeous blaze orange trees, which I could not identify.

"What kind of trees are those?" I asked curiously. "I don't believe I have seen a tree like that."

"Those are pistachio trees. They sure turn a bright orange in the fall."

"I didn't even know they grew around here. Guess I thought they were more exotic," I said ignorantly. I searched my memory in vain for an image of a similar looking tree, but this sight before me was burned into my mind.

"They will grow just fine in these parts. Not too many people know about them I reckon."

At the Piggly Wiggly, we purchased some red potatoes, bacon, onions, and tomato juice before returning to his house. Back inside his house, he went to the cabinets and sought the remaining ingredients needed for the stew.

In the light of the small kitchen window over the sink, Mr. Andrews excitedly said, "Ok, Dr. Curtis, we have everything we need… well almost everything…" He paused and grinned behind his dentures. "I sure hope the catfish are biting," he winked and pointed a thumb over his shoulder in the direction of the pond.

Through the screen door we went down the con-

crete steps with the sharp crack of the door closing behind us, by the pepper plants adorned with color, and
to the kitchen house with its peeling white paint where
we retrieved the fishing poles. The light blue worm can
sat next to the darker blue fish feed container. Mr. Andrews picked up both. There was a light spring to his
step. He seemed younger, more vibrant. We walked down
the grassy slope to the two awaiting metal chairs in the
sun and took our seats. The sky overhead was full of high
altitude, puffy, white clouds with no threat of rain. In
and out the sun would peek from behind the clouds. The
birds sang. The pines whispered. The pecan leaves chat-
tered softly in the subtle breeze. Warm though it was, the
temperature down by the pond was comfortable. In that
moment sitting by Mr. Andrews, a song verse popped
into my head:

> *And somehow I've learned how to listen*
> *For a sound like the sun going down.*
> *In the magic the morning is bringing*
> *There's a song for the life I have found.*
> *It keeps my feet on the ground.*
> (Alan Jackson, "Song For The Life")

As I sat by Mr. Andrews, I listened. I heard the
sounds that were not manmade. Mr. Andrews was listening too. We did not speak, silently observing the moment
around us. I thought how unfortunate it was that many

people could not comprehend a sound like the sun going down. Our world was evolving into a hyperdrive of frenzied efficiency, and it seemed as if there was no turning back.

But there I was, turning back. Slowing the gears of motion. Maybe I was on a raging river facing the current head on determinedly paddling upstream dodging all the others going the way of the rapid flow. I yearned to be different in that respect. To go right when the whole world tried to go left. The life I had found here with Mr. Andrews was simple but so enriched. Simplicity did not imply "easy." Hard work was just as much a part of this lifestyle as love of family. However, there was an appreciation to pause to see life as it was in the moment, to be grounded to this life of dedication as the mighty pecan trees to the hard, red clay, their roots penetrating deep and thirstily to anchor securely.

The first catfish that bit Mr. Andrews' hooked earthworm was dropped into a big blue bucket.

"We need a few more like him," Mr. Andrews remarked.

As if on cue, Mr. Andrews set the hook on another dense catfish. Within fifteen minutes we had our goal.

Weighted down with six slippery, wiggling catfish, the bucket was expectantly heavy as I toted it to the outdoor sink behind the kitchen house.

"Set the bucket there. We are going to clean them in a little bit. I got a hankering for some pepper jelly first." He took his hat off and wiped his forehead with his sleeve.

Inside over our favorite snack and a cold glass of sweet tea, Mr. Andrews recounted his recent trip to Americus, Georgia, to see his great grandson, Andrew, who was two years old.

"That little fella was sitting on the floor playing with letter blocks and picked up the M and said, 'M.' Then he flipped it upside down and said, 'W.' He sure is a smart youngun." He chuckled at the thought, proud as he could be of his great grandson. "You know, Dr. Curtis, I feel mighty blessed to have lived long enough to know my great grandson. I feel like we did a good job of raising Harold into a fine man. Amy and Mark have made me as proud as a granddad can be, and now I have another generation to watch grow. Yes sir, I have been mighty blessed."

Slowly swirling my glass in the water on the table left from the glass's condensation, I reflected on Mr. Andrews' simple life blessings. He did not ask for or expect much. He did not feel as though he deserved anything. Many people feel entitled to things but not Mr. Andrews. Simple... he kept his life simple.

I noticed Mr. Andrews glance down at his silver watch on his right wrist as he said, "It's about time to go clean some fish. I hope you brought a good knife."

He smiled his playful smile because he knew I brought a knife. And not just any knife. The knife I made from the "Carnegie steel" with the small antler handle salvaged from a buck I shot as a kid. My own story was intertwined in this knife, the third and final knife in the "Carnegie steel" set. Now I would begin to imprint more of my life on it by cleaning the first of many catfish with it. Mr. Andrews called it "one mean little fish cleaning knife."

Standing at the outdoor metal sink with a catfish secured to the old hickory board, Mr. Andrews started skinning the fish. He had insisted on cleaning the first one and using my knife.

"Yes sir, you got yourself a fine little knife right here. It doesn't hurt that you got some of the best steel you could ever find."

Just then a white truck wheeled into the dirt driveway. Out stepped Harold with a big smile.

"Hey, Doc! Daddy said you were coming over for his birthday. I hear he's going to cook up some catfish stew."

"His Almost Famous Catfish Stew," I emphasized proudly. The three of us laughed and talked while we filleted all six of the fish.

Harold said, "I just wanted to drop by and say hey. Sorry I can't eat with y'all tonight. We are going to celebrate Friday night. I better get back to work. See you later on, Daddy. And good to see you again, Doc."

When Harold's truck turned out of the driveway, Mr. Andrews spread charcoal in his small grill and lit a match. Next he put the twelve fillets on a piece of tin foil and patiently waited for the grill to get hot.

"I've always preferred the charcoal flavor to gas," he commented with his arms crossed on his chest, staring at the grill. "It's important for the recipe. If you are going to make the Almost Famous Catfish Stew, you gotta do it right." He was smiling. "It's so good, It's almost famous."

When the grill was sufficiently hot enough, Mr. Andrews laid the foil with fillets on the grill rack and replaced the lid to begin smoking the white meat. After a while the fish was ready, and I carefully carried the meat laden foil up the steps, through the screen door, and into the kitchen.

"Alright, Dr. Curtis. Grab that pen and note pad over there. I figure you may want to jot this down."

From memory he began to tell me the recipe. "About three and a half pounds of diced red potatoes, two large diced onions, of course the catfish--I use about four pounds of fillets smoked on a *charcoal* grill, four strips of bacon, four tablespoons of butter, two tablespoons of worcestershire, two teaspoons of seasoning salt, two teaspoons of salt, two teaspoons of garlic powder, one teaspoon of black pepper. Then, you take the potatoes, onions, bacon, and butter in a pot and stir on high, then add 2 quarts of tomato juice plus the other ingredients and bring it to a boil, then back to simmer. Add your catfish in cut chunks while it's simmering. When the potatoes are done, it's ready to serve!"

He licked his lips and made a funny face opening his eyes wide. Taking the red potatoes from the plastic grocery bag, I assisted in cutting them up using a wood handled knife he had made many years before for kitchen use. With watering eyes we diced the two big onions. Placing the chunks of potatoes, onions, bacon, and butter in his large, silver pot, Mr. Andrews turned the stove on to start the cooking process. The bacon's aroma overpowered the other ingredients to fill the small kitchen with a mouth watering olfactory stimulation. The bacon sizzled as Mr. Andrews stirred the pot with a spoon. Picking up the tomato juice, he slowly poured the thick, red liquid in the pot followed by the rest of the ingredients minus the catfish. Bubbles infrequently popped up to the hot liquid's surface, but gradually the bubbles rose in more rapid fashion.

"Ok, Dr. Curtis, it's time for the main ingredient. Add the catfish!" He lightheartedly commanded.

The stew seemed to thicken as he gently stirred. Plopping a soft chunk of potato on a napkin, he let it cool and then took a bite, slowly chewing to assess the texture.

"A little bit longer. Maybe four or five more minutes."

At last the long awaited "Almost Famous Catfish Stew" was ready to serve!

"Go ahead, Dr. Curtis, get the first bowl."

"No sir, it's your birthday. You go first, or at least

let Mrs. Nell go before me."

Mrs. Nell had just shuffled into the kitchen: "You are our guest, Andrew. We want you to go first."

At that Mr. Andrews ladled a large helping into a bowl and stuck the bowl in my hands.

"There you are, Dr. Curtis. Go make yourself comfortable at the table."

Objecting was futile, so I obediently walked to the dining table and set the stew down at my place mat. Mr. Andrews then scooped a smaller amount for his wife and set the bowl at her place. Mr. Andrews walked back to the kitchen and returned holding his bowl of stew. He removed his hat, took his seat at the head of the table, and bowed his head.

"Our most gracious Father, we are humbled by your greatness and your mercy. You have given us more than we deserve, and we will serve you with a loving heart the best that we can. Thank you for our friends and family and the strong love we share. We ask that you bless this food in Jesus Christ's name. Amen."

"Amen," we answered.

I dipped my spoon in the thick, creamy stew, being sure to collect potato and catfish for my first bite. My mouth open wide, I sucked in the spoonful of stew and allowed my taste buds to perform their work. My first impression revealed a highly palatable dish without being overbearing. I could most definitely distinguish the smoked flavor. There was a satisfying fullness, which would cure a hunger. So simple, like his knife making, like his life. But so rich in quality. The way I expected. So many things in life are overdone to outcompete. We feel we must abandon the old for the new, and then suddenly the old is forgotten. This recipe was almost too simple for modern times... almost.

As I let the flavors dance on my tongue, I relished the moment. It is not easy to live in the moment without regard for the future, but sipping on my stew, I achieved just that. The ability to focus on life as it is happening is a gift. However, there is a certain level of responsibility to be able to envision the future and plan accordingly. In our frenetic world, foresight can blind us of the present. As with anything in life, there should exist a balance. Mr. Andrews had figured out the balance, much of which involved simplifying the chaotic system in which we lived.

I looked at Mr. Andrews, then at Mrs. Nell, then at the cozy little dining room with a table, chairs, a wood cabinet at one end, a side table, and a few pictures on the walls. This house, built in the early 1900s, without central heating and air, still provided the Andrews with all that they would need or want. They were proud of what they had and envied no one. It can be stated that the more one possesses, then the more burdens one can feel. It is no wonder that many a wealthy person will escape his mansion and retreat to a small, isolated cabin in the woods to rusticate and to recharge. To downsize. To escape the clutter. To step back in time. To simplify. Even if only for a short while.

"So what do you think, Dr. Curtis? Is it as good as you thought it would be?" Mr. Andrews spoke through a mouthful of stew, raising an eyebrow above his glasses.

"It's even better than I imagined," I answered truthfully before taking another savory bite.

The impression had been ingrained in my memory. This taste... never would I taste this recipe again without experiencing the warm, peaceful feeling that I felt now. It was the lifestyle that I tasted and smelled. Just as his handmade knives allowed me to connect to and feel this extraordinary way of living, so the catfish stew embodied the same olfactory experience, appealing to smell and taste rather than touch and sight.

After the delicious meal, of which I had two helpings, I found myself on the old blue couch again sitting to Mr. Andrews' right.

"I'm mighty proud of my great grandson, and it sure tickles me that they named him Andrew."

"Well, I sure approve of the name," I chimed in, laughing.

"I'm afraid it's a rough world he's been born into. Just hope he stays on a straight path. If he puts God first, then he can't stray too far. You know, Dr. Curtis, there's always been good and evil as long as there's been man. I don't know if there's necessarily more evil now, but the news sure makes it seem that way. We just have to recognize that there is evil out there and be the good that counteracts it. The ironic thing is the evil actually amplifies the good. So the evil always loses."

He smiled slightly and stared at the window; a pecan limb shadow was outlined on the pane in a golden orange from the late afternoon's waning sunlight. Slowly, Mr. Andrews turned left and reached for the drawer, THE drawer, and withdrew a sheathed antler knife, which not surprisingly was one I had not seen before. He freed the snap with a sharp pop and delicately slid the knife from its leather cover. The antler handle was a pale yellow that merged into brown streaks at the base and was ever so noticeably curved downward with a fairly narrow diameter— for a small hand, I thought. The blade was somewhat squat in appearance with a straight spine, no thumb groove. The nickel silver bolster was separated from the handle by his signature red, white, and black spacers. All pieces were deeply polished.

Eyes on the knife, he said in a low voice, "I'm not sure how many more knives I will be able to make. I'm getting old, Dr. Curtis. These hands are stiff and ache all the time. I just can't work on knives like I used to. That's why I decided to go ahead and make Andrew a knife, a keepsake, from his great granddad. Maybe one day he will appreciate having this."

"I'm sure he will. It's a beautiful knife," I added.

Mr. Andrews handed over the knife to me, and I caressed the smooth handle. One day a different Andrew would hold this very knife made specifically for him.

This knife held a story before it would ever reach him. Even I was a part of its story now and perhaps the only person outside the family to know of its existence.

With both hands I delivered the knife back to Mr. Andrews as he safely secured the knife in its protective leather sheath. He then laid the knife in the drawer and pushed the drawer shut.

Leaning back with a sigh, he said, "I'm really glad you came over today. I've been wanting to make you the 'Almost Famous Catfish Stew' for a long time but had to wait for the right special occasion. I'm 84 today, and I don't know if I will see another birthday." He paused and looked at me.

Fidgeting with my fingers, I awkwardly stammered, "Mr. Andrews, you don't look or act 84. I think you got plenty of years left."

A doubtful smile formed on his lips. He could sense my discomfort with the topic.

"Don't worry, Dr. Curtis, it's a part of life. No one makes it out alive. I'm blessed to have lived the life I have, and I wouldn't change anything. No sir, I wouldn't change a thing." I believed those words. The light inside the house now was brighter than outside with the sun already below the horizon. The time had come to make the drive east back to Alapaha.

"Well, Mr. Andrews, it's getting about that time. I really appreciate your sharing your catfish stew recipe with me. It sure was delicious. I see now why it's almost famous!"

We laughed as we both rose to our feet. Saying my goodbyes to sweet Mrs. Nell, my legs automatically carried me through the house to the kitchen, the floor creaking underneath my feet.

Mr. Andrews popped the refrigerator door open and gripped a white Cool Whip container.

"I wanted to send you some stew home for Leigh to try. See what she thinks. It's ok for her to be critical of it. Just remind her it's not famous yet," he playfully chuckled, handing me the plastic container.

Out the small window above the sink, I could barely discern the pecan trees with the pines in the background. Through the short, offset, wooden kitchen door, I pushed onto the tiny screen porch, past the slamming screen door, down the concrete steps, and slowly walked to my truck by the side of the house.

Once at my truck door, I spun around to face Mr. Andrews.

I initiated the departing conversation, "Happy birthday, Mr. Andrews. I really had a good time today, and I'm so glad you shared your 'Almost Famous Catfish Stew' with me."

The air held a slight chill as I stood awaiting a reply, and a crescent moon hung low in the colorful, waning light of the western sky.

Mr. Andrews looked towards the horizon of orange, pink, and purple for a few seconds. "It was a good day…"

We both peered out toward the sky to see the thin moon chase the sun over the treetops.

"It sure means a lot to have you come see me today."

In the dim light it was difficult to tell, but I believe I could see his eyes glisten with tears.

He extended his hand and said, "Come back when you can."

CHAPTER 12:

"You remember that knife I told you about, the one I couldn't find to show you?"

In retrospect, I guess I should have known. The clues were there, but I failed to see, or refused to see, might be the more appropriate phrasing. The mind has a way of distorting the truth at times, especially to align with its desires. Sometimes a person believes only what he wants to believe. I fell victim to this false perception of reality.

Oh--but he knew though. He could feel the change within himself.

The visit began like many others. It was not entirely unusual for Mr. Andrews to not greet me outside when I arrived, especially on this oppressively hot day in late July 2017. I parked my truck where I always had next to the side of the old, white house. Despite being in the truck's air conditioner for nearly two and a half hours, my back was damp with sweat. I stepped out into the mid morning heat and looked up toward the familiar towering pecan trees, whose leaves still boasted a healthy, weighty, green color, not yet tainted from the summer's withering heat. A warm wind blew across the yard, offering no reprieve and whirled amongst the dense foliage above.

I walked the few paces to the concrete steps by the screen porch, and in the shade of the thick shrubs, I saw a shy but curious gray tabby kitten that reminded me of a young Tidbit. It was strikingly similar in pattern except for the lack of a bobbed tail, which was Tidbit's characteristic feature, albeit manmade. Kneeling to the dry grass, I reached my hand out and talked softly to coax the small kitten from its shadowy cover. It meowed, hardly audible to my ears, touched its moist, pink nose to my fingers, and then tilted its head sideways to rub its face against the back of my knuckles. I slowly rose to my feet, the sun beating down mercilessly on my sweaty skin.

"I'll be back, little buddy," I reassured the kitten.

Up the concrete steps, I pushed my way through the screen door and let it slam shut loudly behind me to signal like a doorbell my arrival. I delayed a few seconds and could hear someone stirring inside nearing the door. The old, rickety, metal doorknob rattled briefly, and with a clink allowed the kitchen door to swing open.

"Hey, Dr. Curtis, glad you could make it out today. I've been looking forward to your visit." I smiled, shook his hand firmly, and entered the small kitchen, shutting the door behind me.

"Come on in and sit down," I was instructed.

Mr. Andrews had his boots off, gray socks on his feet, worn, faded blue jeans, a light green short sleeve collared shirt untucked, and no hat on his mostly bald head. I could not recall his ever not wearing a cap except during a meal. I found it unusual this day.

I trailed Mr. Andrews into the sunlit den and greeted Mrs. Nell who was calmly seated in her chair opposite the blue couch. She wore white pants and shirt with colorful flower print. Her white hair looked recently styled, and she appeared beautiful but tired.

I took my seat next to Mr. Andrews on the soft couch. The room was filled with a warm, orange glow from the curtained windows opposite us, but the window AC unit was maintaining a comfortable temperature, humming quietly in the corner. A news channel played on the TV screen with muted sound.

"It feels like July in South Georgia," Mr. Andrews joked in his typical good humor. "You picked a good, hot day to come over. This weather has been keeping me in the house more. I just can't stand the heat like I once could. And these hands of mine sure do ache a lot. See that thumb right there?" He held his left hand up for me to see. "Some days it's so stiff I 'bout can't use it." He took a deep breath and exhaled slowly before continuing, "We are just getting old, Dr. Curtis. I really don't mean to complain though. I've had a good life and wouldn't change a thing. It's a blessing to live as long as I have."

"But you still look great, Mr. Andrews," I tried to

lighten the tone. "You definitely don't look like you are almost 86."

He smiled kindly back at me, but his expression was weak. I had, in fact, noticed that his frame seemed thinner beneath his clothing like he had lost weight. His blue jeans sagged below his waistline even though his belt was cinched on the last hole. His face, paler than I had seen, was slightly sunken in, revealing more prominent cheek bone features.

We continued to chat, mostly about my job. He loved hearing stories of interesting veterinary cases I had encountered. Favorite of all was my story years before about a small monkey, who when agitated, would defecate in his hand and launch warm feces at any poor soul close enough to receive his aim. "Seen any more monkeys lately?" he would often ask, always with a fit of laughter.

At lunchtime the three of us made turkey sandwiches on white bread with mayonnaise and juicy, ripe tomato slices that Mr. Andrews cut with one of his handmade, wood handled kitchen knives.

"These look like some good tomatoes here, Mr. Andrews."

"Oh yes sir, these are my heirloom tomatoes I got out there in the garden."

"I haven't had much luck growing tomatoes," I admitted.

"One thing you might be doing wrong is watering the leaves. Try just watering the roots and keep the plant dry. It doesn't hurt to allow them some shade too, especially to block some of the hot afternoon sun."

I bit into my sandwich tasting the refreshing coolness of the plump tomato slices. My sweet tea was cold and smooth going down. This lunch--so simple, so good, so time defying. The flavor encouraged my mind to reach back in time to when I was a boy sitting at my grandparents' table. Those were fond memories. I appreciated the way that this lifestyle that the Andrews had shared would stall perceptible time for me. No worries for the future, just peaceful, in the moment feelings with a sprinkle of sweet memories of the past.

I noticed Mr. Andrews chewing his food longer than normal and then swallowing with a strained expression. My sandwich was gone, and he was only on his second bite. As he swallowed again, a sudden cough seized him.

Fearing that he was choking, I jumped to my feet, and he nonchalantly waved me away, sputtering, "I'm fine. Just got this dang swallowing problem with my esophagus. Excuse me."

He pushed away from the table to go to the bathroom. I heard the unmistakable sound of his vomiting. He returned to the table, his forehead sweaty, and drank a sip of tea. The partially eaten sandwich remained on his plate.

"I do hope you will stay with us for supper too, Andrew," Mrs. Nell offered in her quiet manner. "Edwin wants to make shrimp creole tonight."

Mr. Andrews nodded his head in agreement. "You do like it, don't you?"

"Yes sir, I love it. But don't feel like you have to feed me."

"You know me by now, Dr. Curtis. I wouldn't do it if I didn't want to," he said through a gracious smile. "Come on, let's run to the store."

The AC in his old S-10 pickup truck was not strong enough to combat the intense July heat, so we manually cranked the windows down for air flow. Though hot, the air felt pleasant whipping through the open windows as we rode the winding country road. There was no way of knowing that this drive would be my last outing with Mr. Andrews, but the memory was imprinted in my mind.

Upon returning from the grocery store, we put away the few purchased items and made our way back to the couch. As Mr. Andrews reached for the side table drawer, my heart fluttered with excitement just like it did the first visit nearly five years before. "The magic drawer," I thought. What kind of knife would he pull out today? The chosen knife was antler handle, indeed, but different from all the rest, for this one folded shut. The rusty blade with the antique appearance told me that this knife was old.

"Wow, did you make this?"

"No, a fellow long ago gave this to me, but he wasn't the one who made it. I wish I knew the story of this ole thing. I guess I never will, but I was told it was most likely the first folding knife ever made. See how the locking mechanism works on the back?" He pointed to a metal piece on the back of the blade. "No, I've never made a folding knife before." He looked lost in thought, rolling the knife over in his stiff, wrinkled hands. "I reckon I never will." Without taking his eyes off the folding knife, he commented matter of factly: "I don't believe I will ever make another knife."

I wanted to cry out in opposition, to say, "Of course you will make more knives! It's what you do. It's who you are." My brain had branded him as a knife maker from our first visit together. But then a guilty sense swept over my foolish thought. Knife making was only a tiny part of Mr. Andrews. He was loving, kind, generous, compassionate, patient, thoughtful, humorous, witty, intelligent, and wise. He was what I wanted to be. The world needed to know this man.

He handed the folding knife to me without a word, keeping it securely locked. I opened the blade and examined it quietly.

"I want you to have it."

"But...," I started to argue but realized it was sense-less to object. "Thank you, Mr. Andrews. I love it."

"I figured you would. I just wish I could tell you its story. Hey, think you got room now for some crackers and pepper jelly?"

At the dining table, I smeared some dark amber jelly on my cream cheese and club cracker. Mr. Andrews cautiously nibbled on a corner of the cracker he had pre-pared and methodically chewed, grinding it firmly with his dentured teeth. Like always during this snack ritual, he spoke admiringly of his family. He coughed a few times mildly after swallowing but experienced no major setbacks.

"We should have some shade now by the pond if you want to go fish a while."

"Yes sir, I would love that," I replied.

At the water's edge, the two metal chairs sat side by side looking out over the calm, green water. Those were our chairs. Countless hours we had sat talking, pon-dering, laughing, listening. Just being in the moment--where time slowed while the world spun ever faster.

There's a song for the life I have found.
It keeps my feet on the ground.

This was the life I loved. The water before us seemed to

dilute the stresses of life. On our walk down to the pond, we had not even bothered to grab our fishing poles. The air was sticky and hot. Hardly a breeze stirred the trees. In the shade, though, the temperature was tolerable. Occasionally, a couple of crows called back and forth in the pine tops. The cows across the road remained quiet and hunkered down in the shade of the oak trees. Thick clouds formed in the distance, but the sky above was open and bright. We sat and we talked. And we watched the world around us at that location, at that point in time. And we listened. We listened to the sun going down. The two of us side by side at the bank's edge.

I'm not certain how long we sat, but eventually we made our way back up the gentle slope one last time to the old white house that was built by his grandparents. Past his pepper plants in their oversized black pots and the enormously tall pecan trees. Past the kitchen house with the uneven steps where we sanded so many blades. Past the group of cats huddled in the shrubs by the concrete steps. Through the slamming screen door and into the house. One last time.

"I really should be making us some Almost Famous Catfish Stew tonight instead of shrimp creole," he said as we stepped through the creaky, offset kitchen door.

"Why?" I asked bewildered. "We can only cook that on a special occasion."

He forced an awkward smile and said, "Shrimp creole it is then."

Looking back on his remark, I assume he thought this to be our last visit, which would have most definitely justified a special occasion for catfish stew. How could I have known?

He cooked while I assisted, and I watched through the small kitchen window as the summer shadows covered the yard outside. When the creole was done, Mr. Andrews served three bowls with mine containing the largest portion. Mrs. Nell came in the dining room from the bedroom and sat down, after which Mr. Andrews and I joined her. Mr. Andrews said the blessing, and we began to eat. Taking small bites, Mr. Andrews strained to get his food swallowed without a coughing fit. I wished I could help, but instead I gulped my meal down with ease, a guiltiness overtaking me.

After supper, Mrs. Nell cleared the table, shuffling to and from the kitchen, while Mr. Andrews and I went to our spots on the blue couch... one last time. Twilight had overtaken the summer day, and the room was dimly lit by one small lamp on the side table. Again, Mr. Andrews reached for the magic side table drawer. I anxiously watched. What could he possibly pull out now? Had he not shown me all the knives in that drawer yet? As if in slow motion, Mr. Andrews' shaky hand lifted a very plain, sheathless knife out for me to see. It was certainly nothing special in appearance-- a thin, straight, heavily rusted blade, a basic tarnished brass bolster, and a straight, sun bleached antler handle. The knife was extremely worn, and the rust was caked on thickly.

"You remember that knife I told you about, the one I couldn't find to show you?"

I was stunned. "Of course I remember the knife! The mule deer antler handle, the one you cleaned so many catfish with, the one you couldn't find . . . the 'Carnegie steel!' I thought I would never see it. Where on earth did you find it?"

He smiled and said, "I actually found it a while back. It had fallen under the outdoor sink and was buried in the leaves. The blade is probably rusted through now."

I could not believe that was the knife that I had literally dreamed about. So simple, yet so reliable, the knife could tell a lifetime of stories. In that moment, I recognized the symbolism. This knife was much like Mr. Andrews himself. The history of the knife overwhelmed me. Mr. Andrews' favorite catfish cleaning knife was so plain on the outside, but so rich on the inside. It was as if it possessed a hidden message. Things are not always what they seem. Mr. Andrews was a hidden gem for me, and I was fortunate to have found him. Without a doubt, I knew what was coming next.

Mr. Andrews handed the knife to me and said, "It belongs to you now. You may be the only one who can fully appreciate this old piece of a knife."

No argument came from my tongue this time. I accepted the gift.

"You know, Dr. Curtis, I'm glad you stuck with

knife making. It has given this old man something to do, something to look forward to."

He talked as if this would be the last visit, but I refused to see. I peeked at my watch--9:30. I had a two and a half hour drive ahead of me and was scheduled to work the next day. Regretfully, I mentioned the time and my need to depart. Mr. Andrews walked me to the kitchen door but no farther. We shook hands there in the doorway of his grandparents' home. It was the first time he had not walked me out to my truck. The handshake was slow and prolonged.

"Come back when you can, Dr. Curtis."

I stepped out of the house-- one last time.

CHAPTER 13:

"Who knows, Dr. Curtis, maybe one day you will make it famous."

For the third time since locking the clinic doors at 12:30, my emergency pager buzzed on my belt. It was nothing more than a typical, crazy Saturday in the veterinary world. Returning the urgent call, I learned that my next patient was a fourteen week old German Shepherd puppy with bloody diarrhea. "Great," I thought after hanging up the phone, "Another poor parvo puppy."

Upon arrival, the puppy was indeed extremely lethargic and weak, so I immediately placed an intravenous catheter to bolus life-saving fluids. Unfortunately, the parvovirus test revealed a positive result compounded by intestinal worms. After placing my patient in the isolation ward, I disinfected the examination table and washed my hands preparing to eat my packed lunch. The time was 3:30 PM on this last day of September, and I desperately wanted to sit down and relax for a few minutes to enjoy my sandwich.

My cell phone suddenly rang in my pocket—" Edwin Andrews," the screen read. I thought of calling him back but instead decided at last to answer the call.

"Hey, Dr. Curtis." His voice sounded weaker than it had during our previous phone conversation two weeks earlier.

"Hey, Mr. Andrews, how you feeling?"

"Oh, I feel fair," he admitted in a low tone. "It's tough getting old, and these hands of mine just don't want to work right anymore. Enough about me. What's going on with you?"

With great willpower I refrained from announcing my wife's pregnancy. We had tried for a baby for a few years, and now after a year of seeing a fertility specialist, we were joyously expecting our first child in the spring of 2018. Since I planned on visiting Mr. Andrews in another few weeks, I decided that I should tell him in person.

"I've just been working. That's kept me plenty busy, but I have still made some time most nights to work on a knife. The handle is out of a beautiful, dark antler I found this past spring at the Botanical Garden in Athens. It's coming along nicely."

Again I chose to withhold information until the next visit. In actuality, this knife I was making would be for my future son. I would tell Mr. Andrews all about it next visit.

"I will bring it in a few weeks for you to inspect."

"I'm sure it's going to be a fine knife," he predicted. "Say, you haven't found a special occasion to make any Almost Famous Catfish Stew yet have you?"

"No sir, I sure haven't. Too bad I can't go over there for your birthday in a couple of weeks. I have to work that day. Otherwise we could have it then."

"I've always loved that recipe--the flavor, but more than that I have loved the process. Catching catfish, using my knife to clean the fish and cut up the potatoes and onions. I used to grow my own red potatoes too. Grilling the catfish outside on charcoal. And finally putting it all together for a special occasion." He paused and sighed deeply on the other end of the phone. "You might find that you want to tweak it a time or two... change it up a little bit. Who knows, Dr. Curtis, maybe one day you will make it famous."

Laughing, I responded, "I don't think that recipe needs changing. It's good enough to be famous now."

"Well, Dr. Curtis, I just wanted to check on you. Come visit me when you can."

"Bye, Mr. Andrews. Thanks for calling. I will see you next month."

Characteristic of all his phone conversation endings, Mr. Andrews never said goodbye. He just hung up the phone. True to my word, I did make the trip to Carnegie to see my old friend one week after his birthday, but the occasion was not what I expected.

CHAPTER 14:

"There's a song for the friend I have found."

"Doc, this is Harold Andrews. I just called to tell you we lost Daddy this morning about four o'clock. If you would, call me when you get this message. Thank you. Bye . . ."

Wednesday, October 18, 2017, I had the day off work. The time was 12:20 PM. I was in the kitchen of my house making a peanut butter and honey sandwich when my phone rang in the den. Checking my phone screen, I saw I missed a call from Mr. Andrews and that there was a voicemail. As I listened to the message, time seemed to slow. Hearing Harold's voice instead of Mr. Andrews' was a sudden shock. I listened to the message twice before setting my phone down on the kitchen counter. I gave reality a chance to intermingle with my emotions. I would never get to hear Mr. Andrews' voice again. Never again would I go to Carnegie to discuss knives, to fish, to eat pepper jelly, to sit on the old, blue couch next to my friend. Never again would I have such a deep relationship with someone fifty-four years my senior. My oldest friend was gone now. As time would pass, I realized that the tables would eventually turn. Gone would be the days that I was a young man in an old man's presence. The torch would pass to me as role of mentor. I smiled at the thought. What incredible, valuable life lessons could I pass on to future generations, lessons graciously passed on to me from Mr. Andrews? Mr. Andrews' life was lived. He had no regrets. And now he would live through a multitude of people he touched. Thankfully, I was one of those people.

Sitting at my kitchen table, I chewed quietly on my sandwich and reminisced, scrolling through my phone to view pictures of my five years with this magnificent man. My phone was full of pictures of our visits in chronological order-by time, dates. Grabbing a pen, I jotted down some of my many memories so as not to forget and to perhaps reference one day to write a book on this special relationship. I had also kept brief notes of most of our visits. I began to realize just how amazing out relationship had been.

The greatest mystery to me was how he sensed when our last visit would be—how he gave me his favorite catfish cleaning mule deer antler knife with the old "Carnegie steel," my most cherished possession of his.

Two days later my wife and I, driving west, came up to the familiar, sharp, left hand curve with the pretty white house. Instead of veering left onto the red clay driveway that went by the small, green pond, I drove my truck slowly past. Another mile down the road, just before the Carnegie intersection with the railroad tracks, a small, white church fitted with stained glass windows appeared on my left not twenty feet off the road-- Carnegie Baptist Church. I parked my truck in a small mowed grassy area next to the church under the shade of a tall pine tree. The cemetery lay directly across the road and overlooked a gentle slope with a field beyond.

Stepping out into the noon sunlight, I felt the heat penetrate into my black dress suit, causing sweat to trickle down my back. Harold had informed me that I was one of the pallbearers, so I had arrived early for the 3 PM service. Meeting the other pallbearers, I realized I was the youngest by several decades.

"You're that veterinarian Edwin made knives with," one of the men remarked.

"No," I thought, "I'm that veterinarian who made knives *with Mr. Andrews*. Better yet, I'm the *boy* who made knives *with Mr. Andrews*." But more importantly, I was his *friend*.

We milled around the church grounds chatting idly while awaiting friends and family to arrive to the small church. Mr. Andrews' close, loving family came early, and for the first time I had the opportunity to meet Amy and Mark, the grandchildren Mr. Andrews and Mrs. Nell had talked of proudly. With the small church filled, the preacher spoke of the incredible life of Mr. Andrews and all that he was. The service was lighthearted, which I had anticipated because of the uplifting effect Mr. Andrews had on everyone in attendance.

I stared at the casket, listening to the kind words being spoken, and thought of a quote by Winnie the Pooh: "How lucky I am to have something that makes saying goodbye so hard."

Following the service, I aided the fellow pallbearers in placing the casket in the rear of the hearse which slowly drove the short distance across the road to the cemetery. I followed behind the shiny, black car feeling the heat of the day pressed on my body, the temperature reminding me more of August than October. A warm breeze blew from the east, and a single, yellow leaf gracefully glided down in the path in front of me, almost within arm's reach. The sun shined brightly, and way off in the distance, I could hear a cow moo.

Reaching to the ground, I lifted the thin leaf and knew at once--pecan. Where had it blown from? How far could this leaf have traveled in the mild wind that blew? Mr. Andrews' house lay not far to the east, within earshot of where I now stood. Turning my face into the breeze, I peered up the road in the direction of the house I loved. I felt as though the leaf was a sign from Mr. Andrews himself to me. With the yellow pecan leaf slipped into my hip pocket, I marched peacefully to the grave site. I faced the family who were seated under the green tent in front of me, and my eyes landed on little Andrew, the precious great grandson. I ached at once, acknowledging my delay to reveal my wife's pregnancy to Mr. Andrews. Had I really been so foolish as to miss my chance? Why hadn't I simply told him on the phone during our last conversation?

My hands plunged deep into my hip pockets, and I felt the delicate, soft leaf against my left thigh. Perhaps Mr. Andrews knew now. My tense muscles relaxed, and I experienced the peace that passes understanding. Now I was certain that he knew. Our friendship was too strong, too pure to be coincidental. I closed my eyes and listened. The sound of the preacher's voice faded. I listened... then I heard it. It was a sound that no one else perceived. It was the sound of the breeze dying down.

I had always thought the first chorus verse of Alan Jackson's song was the most relatable to my relationship with Mr. Andrews, but now it was the final verse speaking to me with only subtle differences to the first.

> And somehow I've learned how to listen
> For a sound like the <u>breeze dying down</u>.
> In the magic the morning is bringing
> There's a song for the <u>friend</u> I have found.
> [He] keeps my feet on the ground.

I opened my eyes to stare out across the gently sloping meadow, a beautiful spot indeed to be laid to rest.

Leaving the cemetery, I decided to pull by the pond one last time. The pond's surface rippled slightly, signaling a soft breeze in the air. The orange light of the sun was more angled now, reflecting an intense glow on the surrounding trees. The tops of the pines ever so slowly swayed. Even though I was in my truck, I knew the sound. I could see it.

A fish swirl toward the middle of the pond caught my attention. Then I saw the two metal chairs side by side, waiting... waiting. Those were our chairs.

And suddenly I was back. There we were together. Mr. Andrews on the left and I on the right. Tidbit standing attentively at the base of Mr. Andrews' chair flicking his tail while watching the pond before him. The song of the mourning doves sweeping through the pines. The cows mooing across the road, their voices echoing in the oak bottom. So clearly I could hear the pecan leaves rustle high above. No man made sound was heard. The moment was frozen in time. No erasing that.

An indescribable peace overtook me knowing that this was not fantasy. Before me lay the truth, the life I searched for and found. There it was before me unfolding like a song. Mr. Andrews and me, our friendship strong and deep and real.

Then I hummed the final two lines of the melody in my head.

There's a song for the friend I have found.
[He] keeps my feet on the ground.

He keeps my feet on the ground.

CHAPTER 15:

"The Special Occasion."

I double check to be sure I have what I need. The small red potatoes and the two large onions rest on the counter. From the kitchen of my new home, I gaze across the bright den to the expansive, white book-shelves mounted on the opposite wall, sunlight pouring in through the sky-light windows above. Five shelves up, perched to the right of the TV sits an old, worn out knife on a small display stand made of whitetail antler and driftwood. There is nothing ornate about this knife-- a rusty, whittled, straight blade, a plain brass bolster fully tarnished, a small, straight, sun-bleached antler handle. That's all there is to it, to the eye. But, oh what stories this knife can tell, beginning long before my time here on Earth. One story I know well. It's the story of a young man searching for something in life. He knows not what he is searching or even that he is searching at all, until he meets an old man who teaches him about a way of life worth living. That moments are what matter most, where one neither looks to the past nor the future. And that peace can be found in the simplest of ways, a simplicity, which surrounds us all but is often obscured by the accelerated pace of life.

I push through the screen door of the porch to my white house and down the brick stairs, the sun's glare forcing my hand up to shield my eyes. The air is cool in the shade but warm in the sunshine, one of those days signaling the arrival of fall. The mourning doves high in the pine tops hoot their soothing song to each other as cows moo in the distance, echoing through the hardwood bottom down the hill. Several towering pecan trees stand sentry in the yard watching over my home, my barns, and the tiny work shed, their leaves turning a brilliant yellow on the limbs. Ringing the pecan trunk, daffodil bulbs hide dormant in the cooling earth awaiting their cue to spring forth from the ground.

I tread past the vacant garden to the work shed where my fishing tackle is stored in one corner near my sanding belts. Picking up my black tackle box and brown fishing pole that Mr. Andrews had given me, I start out down the three wooden steps, walking around the side of the outdoor fish cleaning sink with an old hickory board resting on top. Next to the sink in a white bucket is a blue can of worms. I grab the bucket handle in my right hand and tote my fishing gear in my left. A chatty crow lands in the tall pecan tree with a barely visible white crescent moon in the bright blue sky behind it. I glance at the big black pot holding the prolific pepper plant on the back side of my shed and smile. Though I am not in Carnegie, Georgia, I can see all the resemblances. Mr. Andrews is indeed here.

Down the slope of the hill, I go to the grassy bank of the small pond. The smooth, reflective surface reveals a near mirror image of the deep blue sky and bordering trees with amazing clarity. A single, metal chair patiently awaits my arrival. One day it will not be alone.

Taking my seat, I stare out at a few wispy clouds far off towards the horizon. With a little luck, I will return to my house with the final ingredient for supper tonight. My right hand caresses the smooth antler handle of the small knife attached to my belt.

"Mr. Andrews, it sure is a mighty fine day for your Famous Catfish Stew... after all, it is October 13. Happy Birthday..."

Please visit my website to view more pictures of Mr. Andrews and some of the knives that we made:

andrewcartercurtis.com

Pictures by Haley Skye Photography

If you enjoyed reading my book, then please go to Amazon.com, search for *Famous Catfish Stew*, and leave a review!

Acknowledgements

Publishing a book is a team effort. I never could have imagined how many people would play a role in helping me to succeed. A special thanks goes to the numerous people who offered sincere advice and feedback to guide me along the path.

My mom, Viki Curtis, and sister, Sally Bartlett, were the most instrumental in keeping my dream alive. I take for granted their intelligent wisdom. They were there through all the many drafts, the proof-reads, the marketing process, and the dreaded proposals.

I am truly grateful to my editor, Lydia Rogers, for the invaluable encouragement and confidence in my writing style. She showed me who I am as a writer.

A heartfelt thanks to:

Henrietta Tharpe, an avid reader who voiced an honest opinion early in the process.

Jeff Miller, who graciously offered his years of business expertise to a "stranger" in me.

Ann Carter, a true friend devoted to my book's presentation and marketing.

Cole Barfield, my best friend, for always providing sound legal advise.

Haley Waites, for her generosity and expert photography skills to help bring the story more life.

Stacy Dowdy, for allowing me to share a piece of her heartache.

Mark Davis, without whom I never would have had this story to tell.

Amy & Mark, who were so kind and helpful during the process and for being genuinely excited about my telling their family's story.

Harold, who always treated me like a family friend and who recognized the deep friendship that his dad and I developed.

And of course, to Mr. Andrews and Mrs. Nell, who gave this boy more than he sought to receive. And, for sharing the secrets of the Famous Catfish Stew!

.

ABOUT THE AUTHOR

Andrew Carter Curtis

Andrew was born in south-west Georgia. His love for animals and nature led him to the field of veterinary medicine. Andrew received degrees in Animal Health and Doctor of Veterinary Medicine from the University of Georgia. He currently practices medicine and surgery in Valdosta, Georgia, and lives in a small town with his wife and two young  sons. Hobbies include fishing, hunting, biking, gardening, reading, and knife making.

Andrew is currently working on another book about his friendship with an elderly lady and her dog.

Made in United States
Orlando, FL
23 November 2021

10648719R10105